D1518266

Some Other Words

An Illustrated Anthology

WINDMORE
FOUNDATION
FOR THE ARTS

NATIONAL
ENDOWMENT
for the ARTS
arts.gov

VIRGINIA
VCA
COMMISSION FOR THE ARTS

Published by:
Windmore Foundation for the Arts, Inc.
P.O. Box 38
Culpeper, VA 22701
(540) 547-4333
www.windmorefoundation.org

"Windmore Foundation for the Arts encourages a lifelong passion for the arts by providing a culturally rich and immersive experience for people of all ages."

The views expressed in these materials represent the opinions of the respective authors. Publication of these materials does not constitute an endorsement by Windmore Foundation for the Arts, Inc. of any views expressed herein, and Windmore Foundation for the Arts, Inc. disclaims any liability arising from any inaccuracy or misstatement.

Cover and text design and composition by Caryn Block and Fran Cecere.
Cover Image © Les Walters
Edited by Fran Cecere

ISBN—13: 979 - 8353859178
ISBN—10: 8353859178

Library of Congress Number: 2022917446

Printed in Culpeper, Virginia - United States of America

Contents:

Dedication

This book is dedicated to Past and Present Pen-to-Paper Writers who have shared their memories, their imaginations, and their talents. Without their support this anthology would not have been possible.

Acknowledgments

The Anthology Committee would like to thank the writers who submitted their poems and stories to this anthology. The committee members, listed alphabetically, are: Caryn Block, Fran Cecere, Sally Humphries, Gail Matthews, Gwen Monohan, Bruce Van Ness, and Leilani Worrell.

Our illustrators added so much value. We thank Les Walters for his work on the cover and the story illustrations. Fran Cecere, Caryn Block, Sally Humphries, Gail Matthews, and Leilani Worrell also worked to enhance the stories with pictures or graphics. Jen Poteet, Laurie Rokutani, and Michele LeBlanc-Piche contributed their art for creative illustrations. Caryn Block took on the marathon mission of formatting the pictures, the stories and the publishing. Fran Cecere took the lead as Editor of the book. We greatly appreciate the time and energy they took with these tasks and we also acknowledge their families who supported them. Gail Matthews compiled and edited the biographies.

We thank Windmore Foundation for the Arts, Inc. for their continued support with the publishing of this anthology. Special thanks to the Culpeper County Library for the years of support of our writers' group. The library also gives special recognition to our authors with a Local Authors shelf. We appreciate their encouragement. Pen-to-Paper continues to meet at the Culpeper Library on the first Tuesday of every month at 10:00 AM and 5:00 PM.

All the profits from this book will be given to Windmore Foundation for the Arts, Inc. so they can continue to support Pen-to-Paper in the future.

CELEBRATION

Inspiration,
surprising visits,
lights in the dark
and paths to follow.

Figure 1 Illustration Bobbie Troy

Poetry Is
Bobbie Troy

a flower bloomed
a state of mind
words from the heart
and the soul

a revelation
an inspiration
words from today
and yesterday

a light in the dark
a path to follow
words to teach
and to reach

an emotion felt
a mirror on self
words to last
in the universe

Clever Kendra
Lois Powell

I looked at the dress hanging on my closet door. Mom and I had shopped for weeks. It was perfect. I loved the color. The sales lady said the color was called Shimmering Mint Green. The full chiffon skirt, wide satin sash tied in the back, and the sleeveless top with the scooped neckline made me feel like a princess when I had it on. The length was perfect, just above my knees. Having my hair pulled back in a banana comb with the curls twirling down made me feel so grown up. The eighth-grade graduation dance was tonight. At first my girlfriends and I were going together but then we changed our minds. We decided if a boy asked any of us to go, we'd say yes. After all, it was our first formal dance. Terrel had asked me. I was so thrilled I could barely speak. He was cute and a good dancer.

"Kendra, have you started getting dressed yet? Terrel will be here before you know it. Give me a shout if you need any help," said Mom.

"Okay!" I yelled back. I didn't want any help. Not tonight. I wanted to see my family's faces after I was all dressed. The reason was, I never wear dresses or skirts. Mom says I'm a Tom Boy. I love to play all kinds of sports so I always wear pants, T-shirts, and sneakers. There's nothing like a fast-moving game of soccer. It gets me excited just thinking about it. I play with my girlfriends or with the boys. I love playing with the boys because they hate it when I can get the ball from them or make a goal when they try so hard to block the ball. Yeah! You gotta love it. As I looked at the dress, I was thinking, getting all dressed up including heels may be harder than beating boys in a soccer game.

I had already taken my shower and put lotion on my body from head to toes. I also put on perfume. I borrowed Mom's. I don't own any. I mean, really, why would I. Well, the moment had come. I gently took the dress off of the hanger and carefully eased it over my head. Even though I still had the shower cap on, I made sure I didn't mess up my hair. I tied the sash in the back, put on my pearl earrings and my necklace with the one pearl and slipped into my high heels that Mom had dyed to match the dress. Perfect! I wanted to run but I walked into my parents' room to see how I looked in their full-length mirror. As I was walking into the room, I noticed the dress felt a little snug around the waist. Could I have gained weight since we bought the dress? Nah! As I stood in front of the mirror, I gave the dress a little tug at the waist. RIP! "OH NO!"

"Kendra, is everything okay?" asked Mom. I didn't realize I had said it that loud.

"Uh, yeah, sure," I said.

"All right! I don't know why you don't want any help."

"Because I have my reasons."

"Fine."

I twisted and turned looking in the mirror trying to find the rip. There it was. I had ripped the dress at the waist. It wasn't that bad but you could see it. Now what was I going to do? I untied the sash and started playing around with it to see if I could cover the tear. I tried looping it, folding it. Then I thought of twisting it but I didn't want a wrinkled sash. I looked through Mom's junk tray in her drawer and found some Crazy Glue. Maybe this would help.

Ding! Dong! Oh no, is Terrel here already?

"Kendra, Terrel is here."

"Okay, Mom. I'll be right down."

I finally figured out how I could fix the rip. Rushing into my bedroom, I grabbed my bag and headed down the stairs. When I got to the bottom, I stopped, took a deep breath. Then walked into the living room where everyone was waiting.

"WOW!" said Terrel.

"Honey, you look beautiful," said Dad.

"Oh, yes you do. You certainly aren't my Tom Boy tonight," said Mom.

Even my pain in the neck, twelve-year-old brother said I looked great. All I could do was smile. I couldn't stop smiling. This was what I was hoping for.

"Thanks everyone." Terrel walked to me and gave me my corsage. Mom helped me pin it on.

"Thank you, Terrel. You look great too."

"Thanks, Kendra." Gosh, we sounded so formal.

"Come on, let me take your picture before you leave," said Dad.

We went and stood in front of the fireplace. While we were standing there, Mom kept looking at me.

"Kendra, why is your sash like that?" asked Mom.

"Oh, um, I thought I would try something different."

"Well, it looks quite attractive tied to the side."

"Thanks."

Boy, did I breathe a sigh of relief. As we rushed out the door, I just knew we were going to have a ball. I could just feel it. Terrel's parents were driving us. They're a lot of fun.

"Have a great time," my family said waving from the door.

"Thanks, we will," Terrel and I said together.

"We're going to have a great time," said Terrel.

"You bet," I said as my fingers touched the lump of Crazy Glue and I thought, sash don't fail me now.

Figure 2 Photo Fran Cecere

My Favorite Vacation
Fran Cecere

In 2003 my husband bought a 36-foot motor home. He did all the driving and I did the cleaning and cooking. Roy had a plan about what routes we would take on our trips across country. I checked the internet and travel books to find the best places to visit along the way. We saw many of the National Parks, tourist attractions, and towns which were colorful and interesting. However, one stop really surprised me.

In May, 2016, we made a three-week trip. While in Tennessee, Roy suggested that we go to Graceland. Elvis was a star when I was growing up. I enjoyed his movies and music, but I was not a groupee. I agreed to go to Graceland because Roy wanted to go. We camped in the Graceland RV Park. It was just steps from the mansion.

On Tuesday morning we walked to the main entrance and looked at a huge sign which listed entrance fees to tour the grounds. There were six options stating what we could visit and the different prices. We had no idea which option we should choose. Two ladies stood behind us and discussed that their tour bus driver told them to choose option 2 which was moderately priced and we would still see everything on the grounds. It also included a trip to Beale St. and Sun Studios. I felt if it was good enough for them it was okay with me.

I was enthralled by the entire tour of the home, the grounds, and the museum rooms. Elvis's daughter really honored her father by preserving his memory. There are rooms for his gold records, his colorful outfits, and even copies of the checks showing how much money he gave to charity.

The rooms in the house reflected the very masculine side of Elvis and the very feminine side of Priscilla. The "man cave" had a large pool table and the worst wall paper I have ever seen. Other rooms had stained glass art, a piano, or crystal, along with elegant furniture. On the open areas of Graceland there were horses, Elvis's cars, and his airplanes. Roy and I talked about how much grandeur Elvis had and yet how lonely and sad he was.

While waiting for the bus to take us to the rest of the places, we walked through the lobby of the Heart Break Hotel next to the Mansion.

Our tour also included a trip to Sun Studios where Elvis and many other singers of his time recorded. The tour guide pointed out the pictures taken during recording sessions and the displays of hit records. The studio had not changed.

The next part of the tour was a trip to Beale Street. We were given plenty of time to visit all of the stores before we had to return to Graceland. The entire day will always be one of the best trips we ever had. I was pleasantly surprised. On the bus back to the Mansion a woman and I started talking about Elvis and Graceland. We wondered if our grandchildren's generation would still want to visit the "King's" home and if they didn't, what would happen to Graceland. I hope it will always be a museum honoring Elvis.

The Best Worst Birthday Ever
Gail Matthews

Figure 3 Photo Gail Matthews

It was just going to be the worst birthday ever and there was nothing I could do to stop it. It was going to be more embarrassing than peeing the bed.

Virginia, Aunt Thelma's daughter, had decorated the dining room the day before the party. The Sunday-best lace tablecloth with roller coaster swirls which was usually reserved for preacher dinners signaled the importance of the occasion. Store bought birthday plates, matching napkins, plastic cups and utensils waited in anticipation. Red and white crepe paper streamers twisted together were attached to the ceiling light over the table and the lines secured at each corner of the table. Clusters of colorful balloons completed the decor. All of that was fine and met with my five-year-old approval.

The disaster was happening in the kitchen. Aunt Thelma was making a homemade pound cake and seven-minute frosting. Everyone, who knew anything, knew you had to have a sheet cake from the bakery for a child's birthday party, not homemade. That would be embarrassing enough, but what went on next was mortifying.

Stunned, I watched her divide part of the batter into three small bowls before pouring most of the batter into the circular cake pan. She squeezed drops from the little plastic bottles of food coloring. Drop, drop, drop. The batter in one bowl was tinted red, another green and the last blue. Then she spooned dollops of the tinted batters into the middle of the plain batter. Using a knife, she gently dragged the blade through the tinted dollops. I was horrified at the thought. *The inside of my cake was going to look like mud. The cake was ruined; my party was ruined. She had lost her mind and everyone at the party was going to be a witness.*

My face was red hot with anger, fists clenched, tears streaming down my face. I cried, "How could you!" Tired and "tried" from my whining, she ordered me out of the kitchen, "Go out in the yard and play. Now."

The next time I saw the cake it was iced, curls and peaks of seven-minute frosting hiding the catastrophe. Maybe we could just not have cake.

Too soon, friends from my kindergarten class and several cousins arrived, the song was sung, the candles extinguished, and it was time to cut the cake. No escape. Aunt Thelma asked me for my plate. I passed it to her and looked away when she handed me the first slice. The children gasped looking at the cake on my plate. Then I looked too. The design looked like a red bird in a tree.

All the children pushed their plates forward, clambering to get the next slice. That was a blue bunny! Turning the plates in every direction, each slice was a new design that peaked my guests' imaginations. A green frog. A red dragon. Two red fish in a blue pool. One girl said she didn't want to eat her slice because she wanted to save it to show her mom. Aunt Thelma assured her she could eat her slice and she'd cut another slice to take home for her mom. It was like each guest got a unique gift. What fun!

My mad turned to glad. The cake was a hit and I was proud of my aunt's culinary "*art*." All of that effort and expense was her special gift of love to me.

Figure 4 Photo Gail Matthews

"Everything will be alright in the end so if it is not alright, it is not the end."

Deborah Moggach, *The Best Exotic Marigold Hotel*

Green Jacket #5
Allita Irby

"Epic" is one word to describe it!

Today is Palm Sunday, two thousand nineteen, April 14!

This day, Tiger Woods wins the Masters Tournament in Augusta Georgia!

He is back after twenty-two years!

We see him on film hugging his dad, Earl (2005)!

Today Tiger hugs his son, Charlie (2019)!

Jack Nicklaus said, "I'm so happy for him"

Home for the Holiday
Fran Cecere

When I was thinking about this I couldn't decide how to define "Home." Should I write about the town where I was born or the wonderful home my husband and I have here in Culpeper, Virginia. I wish I could say that I decided by doing Rock, Paper, Scissors and letting that challenge decide for me. However, I'm going to write about my birth place, Utica, New York because of the fond memories I have of it.

In the late 1940s Utica was a town with a hundred thousand people. There were many factories and a booming down town area. My parents owned a restaurant and worked seven days a week. Dad was a great cook of any kind of food but his specialty was Italian food. Mom cooked also, but dad had to season everything.

We lived on the east side of town. It was only blocks away from the center of town. We could walk to pastry shops, department stores, fancy places to eat, or mom and pop pizza stores. Schools were small and the school I attended was only three blocks from home. We never worried about walking alone at night. We would ride our bikes or roller skate from morning to dark and feel safe no matter how far away we were from home.

So for many years, when I thought about going Home for the Holidays, it was returning to my first home, shopping at great bakeries, pizza stores, and other places where we could buy Italian or Polish products. There was a certainty that the food would always taste like it did generations ago and the gifts bought there would be made of the highest quality. Now I walk those streets whose memories are hidden in corners of my mind. In part of my brain, I preserved the smell of the food made in my home town restaurants. The fragrances come forward when I need them.

Returning to Utica also meant that I could visit my cousins, aunts and uncles, and neighbors who loved me. I also could attend mass in the church just two blocks from our old home and see lifelong friends and the Priest who baptized me.

But I don't go to Utica for the Holidays anymore. If I visit the city now it is to return to the bakeries for the cookies, pastry, and tomato pie that are still made from the original recipes. The taste of the food always brings me back to the celebrations my family had and I feel so close to them even though many of them are gone.

Now my Holidays are spent in my home in Culpeper. I cook the traditional foods and invite my family to come to celebrate and share the love together. I serve some of the Polish and Italian meals and continue the traditions that started in Utica. We also attend mass together and pray that we will have many years to come. All the Holidays are blessed because we are together.

ANIMALS

Treasured memories of furry companions who wordlessly touched our hearts and taught us time is precious.

Figure 5 Photo Caryn Moya Block

Summer Love and Dog Days
Bruce Van Ness

Summer love and dog days . . . with whom could they be more closely associated than to our Presley? We first saw the rascally, black and white mixed breed dog, with thick carpeted hair squatting on the Animal Shelter float prior to the start of the Memorial Day parade. My youngest daughter's coaxing guided him over to us to make his acquaintance, and perhaps get a biscuit.

While she brushed Presley's fur with her fingers, he licked my hand, and looked up at me with big, Pixar eyes that implored me to take him home.

"I love this dog," I whispered to my wife. "If we ever get one, I want one just like him."

I liked dogs, just didn't love them, or the work involved with their care. *I figured, what were the chances? It certainly wasn't going to be this time.*

Some months later, again at the pleas of my daughter, we visited the animal shelter up on the hill, "Just to say hello to the animals," according to her insistent voice. When we neared the building, who was bounding down the hill to greet us, but none other than the dog we met months ago. He was joyfully barking as if to say, "I've been waiting for you. What took you so long?"

My wife looked at me . . . Well?

We took him home, loved him and named him Presley. He was like our flesh and blood, and he loved us, well . . . like we were his flesh and blood. He was an exuberant, nose-nudging extrovert who never failed to saturate us with his unconditional love.

Presley and I bonded like two souls who were fated to fill that niche of love that makes two individuals inseparable buddies for life. We ran together, played ball together, and slept together. He was on the floor beside the bed until it was time to lick me awake in the morning.

At dinner time he would promptly arrive at my chair, put his head on my lap and look at me with his "aw, come on" eyes as he tacitly pleaded for some table scraps that I would "sneak" to him under my wife's scolding stare.

Being very sociable, Presley greeted people with a welcoming bark and a wag of his tail. "No need to fear this fella. Just loves people," I would say. At parties and family get-togethers, he wanted to be the center of attention. He would interrupt conversations by squatting back on his haunches and barking just once to announce, "Yup, I'm here. Just love me."

Now once in a while, Presley's mischievous side would show up, and he could be downright obstinate. One time he decided to go deer hunting by himself. We called and called for him, but to no avail.

"He'll be back," I reassured my family. "He just needs a little time to himself." Sure enough, two hours later he came back, panting, glassy-eyed, and with what I swear looked like a silly ass grin on his face.

One night, eight years into our relationship, he got fearfully sick with bloat, hacking and whining in pain. I raced through traffic lights, red or green, as if he was my pregnant wife who needed to get to the hospital. Emergency surgery fixed him that time. Several years later, a recurrence wrested him from us, and left a hole in my heart.

To this day, I still see him galloping across the front lawn to play catch, or running ahead of me in the park. Then he would stop to look back, and intimate with those big Pixar eyes, "Come on, you can do it. Catch up to me."

Kitty Tales
Allita Irby

I am your spirit animal.
I am your guide through life.
I am your baby when you have none.
I am your partner when you want one.
And when I no longer hear or see you,
I will walk beside you from memory.
And when I am no longer in this world,
I will watch over you from the stars.

Figure 6 Illustration Sally Humphries

Herbie in the Dryer
As told by Cally, the Calico Cat, to her staff,
Sally Humphries

My friend Herbie has a fondness for warm places to sleep. In truth, we all like warm places. I confess if I find a patch of sunshine anywhere in the house, I'm on it in the blink of an eye.

On frigid nights I snuggle with my human. It's especially wonderful because she usually puts a warm rice bag under the covers, and I benefit secondhand. I know of a cat who was housed on a screened-in porch and given an electric heating pad to bed down with. She said it was better than nothing but lacked the human smell and touch.

Gracie, a black and white friend of mine who lives in Indiana, tells me the top of the fridge is also a delightfully warm place. She can make it there with one quick leap from the kitchen counter top when her human is busy with the dishes. Not only is it warm, she says smugly, but she is totally out of reach. Which means she can choose to catch a nap, or spend the time thinking things through.

Herbie has tried them all, and in his professional heat-seeking opinion, a clothes dryer with a load of warm towels is the best of the best. The night he found a load of warm towels at exactly the right temperature, he climbed right in, judging the household to be sound asleep. Most were. But not all.

The Mama human had come home late and found a note asking her to finish drying the clothes. Automatically she closed the dryer door and pushed the "ON" button. Boom, Thud, Thud. "Oh rats!" she muttered. "I told those kids not to put their tennis shoes in the dryer."

When she opened the door to fetch the shoes, she was flabbergasted to find a shell-shocked Herbie. His fur was badly rumpled, his whiskers wilted, and his eyes not entirely focused. She told him how sorry she was. She hugged him. She kissed him, and although he seemed to accept her apologies, he was not quite as cordial for some months.

It took time to recover. But he did recover and lived a long, full life as a family favorite.

Still, I think I'd go with the top of the fridge if a patch of sunshine isn't available. The possibility of a dryer tumble is beyond my comfort zone.

Purrfectly yours, Cally

Check It Out

Fran Cecere

Years ago, I watched a very funny comedian performing a three minutes set about the crazy women in scary movies. In his skit he explained that a tiny blonde girl is usually alone in a deserted house. She hears a strange noise and goes into the garage or the basement to investigate. Her only weapon is a flashlight with a battery that shorts out before she can identify the source of the noise. The male comedian then said, "Not me. If I hear a strange noise, there's no way I'm sticking around to find out what it is. I've seen the movies and it's never anything good."

When I watched this comedy routine, I thought I would never do what the dumb blond did. I am educated about the dangers in life and would do whatever I could to protect myself. I never feared for my safety.

Our home in Culpeper has an attached two-stall garage. We park our car and our pickup truck in there. Everyone enters and exits our home using the walk-in garage door and then up two small stairs into our kitchen. We close the double overhead door, but leave the walk-in door partially open so the cat can come in or go out freely. We also have a small refrigerator and a full freezer against the back wall. I can't count the number of times I go through the garage every day.

We were in the midst of the Corona Virus pandemic and stayed at home or social distanced. June 7, 2020 was a perfect spring day. A gentle breeze helped to cool the air and the sky was a brilliant blue. I walked in the driveway for about five minutes talking on the phone to one of my friends. I checked on the growth of our flowers and marveled at how green the woods surrounding our house had become.

When we finished our conversation, I went inside to start to prepare dinner. Since I needed vegetables for what I was making, I went to the freezer in the garage to get them. I was only in the house a few minutes. My daughter phoned as I began to cook dinner. Suddenly I heard noise in the garage. My husband Roy was working on his computer, but I didn't see the cat anywhere. I wondered what the cat was doing to make so much noise. Still holding the phone talking to my daughter, I opened the kitchen door. In the garage, just two feet away from me, was a black bear with its back to me, standing on its hind legs clawing at the closed walk-in garage door. It was about six feet tall, bigger than the door. His paws looked bigger than dinner plates. As his long claws came down, he ripped pieces off the window pane. He was panting, drooling, trapped, and frightened.

Immediately my heart began pounding in my chest. I quickly realized the bear had no way to get out. I slammed the door and screamed into the phone, "There's a bear trapped in our garage."

My daughter calmly said, "Mom, you need to hang up and take care of this."

My heart was racing but my thoughts were clear. I sprang into action. My words ran into one another as I shouted, "Roy, there's bear in our garage. He's trapped. Both doors are closed. We have to get the overhead door open to let it out." I don't know how I was able to think clearly. Both cars were in the garage and they had garage openers. The button to open the garage was on the wall two inches from the bear's massive claws.

Roy looked at me as if I was insane. I think it took him a moment to comprehend what I was yelling. "Roy, go out the front door. Go into our RV. Get the door opener. Open the door. Run!" I demanded.

When he ran out the front door, I looked for my phone so I could try to take a picture. From inside our house there was no clear view of the area just outside the garage.

Roy was in the RV across the driveway from the garage. He pressed the button to open the overhead door. As soon as it rose up high enough, the bear ran out. Even though Roy had the perfect vantage point to take a picture, and he had his phone on his belt, he never thought about using the camera. I ran outside but the bear had already disappeared into the woods. We had no pictures.

When we looked at what happened in the garage, we determined that the bear had walked through the open door, but then went behind it and knocked over two small plastic containers. The bear probably backed into the door causing it to close. That blocked its only means of escape. He also went to a window that was partially open and clawed at it, but all he managed to do was close the window. He returned to the door and frantically attacked it. That was the noise I heard.

My adrenaline high lasted for at least an hour. I rambled on about what I saw, repeating the story to my daughter and to Roy. Even though we don't have a picture we can show to other people, every day when I walk out of the kitchen door, I can still see the bear standing two feet away from me trying to get out of the garage.

I know that if the bear had been on the far side of the garage I would have walked out and looked around for the source of the noise. It makes me cringe to think that I could have been face to face with a terrified bear. I don't even want to imagine what it could have done to me in its agitated state.

My daughter made me laugh about it. I said that I was face to face with a bear and she said, "No, you were face to back with the bear and he must have been "in-bare-assed" for the position he was in.

After the event:
I shared this story with one of our friends. He wrote that it really made him think, and that the story touched on a difficult theme in our lives. We each want to think our lives are secure. Each time we open a door, the view will be, more or less the same. This is an illusion, an artifice we create to convince ourselves we sail in safe waters.

He continued to explain that in my situation of the bear in the garage when I opened the door and instantly that artifice was shattered. Self-preservation demands you believe it was "one off," never to happen again. In truth, each time you open the door, the bear awaits.

Yet again it was an adventure which happily ended well. As much as we fear the door, how sad it would be if each time we opened it we saw the same thing. We just learn to deal with what the other side of the door shows us.

Figure 7 Photo Les Walters

Mr. Big Eyes
Gary Misch

Mr. Big Eyes was a good size orange tom cat with the typical striped tail of a Syria cat. He showed up one day at the feral colony that I feed at Graves barn in downtown Syria, Virginia. He was just as feisty as you'd expect a youngish tom to be. He'd hang back while I fed the females, then stroll in to help himself after I'd gone. There was only one thing for me to do; I trapped him and sent him off to be neutered. It was easy. In retirement I had become a trapper for a trap/neuter/return organization. As the live trap slammed shut Mr. Big Eyes jumped and squirmed furiously, but he was caught. The next day he returned none the worse for wear, but minus his reproductive equipment.

It usually takes a week or so for the testosterone to work its way out of a cat's system, but Mr. Big Eyes came back from the clinic a changed cat. He was immediately friendly, having lost that stand-offish attitude completely. The day after I released him back to the colony, he began rubbing up against me as soon as I showed up with the daily food. After a while he wouldn't eat until I had kissed him on the head. He and I became fast friends. He even had a girlfriend. He always dined with Allison, a blond cat whose litter mate had been adopted by a friend.

Four years into our relationship I arrived on a winter's day to find Mr. Big Eyes meowing like a fog horn. He seemed to be developing an upper respiratory infection. A few days later he had lost the strength to climb the eighteen inches onto the loading dock where the cats ate. Although this is a feral colony, four of the cats can be handled. They act more like pets than feral animals, but they aren't pets. Unlike pets, they don't have health insurance. But I couldn't let my buddy get worse, and possibly die.

I drove home to fetch a cat carrier, but by the time I returned the cats had finished eating, and had scattered. I called out to him. At first Gray Kitty came out to investigate all the noise. Finally, Mr. Big Eyes came slowly strolling out from underneath the loading dock. Was I glad to see him! I kept calling "come on, Mr. Big Eyes," and he followed me right to the truck, where I had the carrier. I picked him up by the scruff of the neck and slipped him in the top of the carrier. The ease with which I was able to do that without a struggle told me how sick he was.

I got an appointment at a twenty-four-hour emergency vet clinic in Charlottesville, where they told me he was pretty sick, but there was a fifty-fifty chance he would recover. I would need to keep him in a warm place for at least a week. I told the vet I would heat up my workshop and keep him in a cage in there until he was well enough to rejoin the colony. He spent the next three nights in our bathroom, and began a slow, steady recovery. Our other cats found him a curiosity, but his health soon declined and he slept most of the day.

On his next vet visit we learned that his lungs were failing, and he had to be euthanized to prevent further suffering.

Change of Tune
Gwen Monohan

Mockingbirds harmonize in trees,
　　　　singing many scores.
Arranging nests and guarding them
　　　　from prowling mischief-makers.

Our cat is playing in the grass,
　　　　stalking any movement.
Caroling birds, chipmunks, moles.
　　　　Even once a dancing toad.

Yet this mother bird flies solo.
　　　　Prefers instead to fight.
Refraining first with raucous chirps.
　　　　Then dive-bombs the cat.

Previously printed on Vox Poetica 2018

Figure 8 Photo Les Walters

Of Course, It's From My Point of View. I'm a Cat.

Fran Cecere

When my feline mother thought we were old enough to leave her, she escorted us to a room with a large open door. My sister and I pranced in and waited to see what would happen. I was better at hiding than she was. My sister chose to wander and leave the big room and I never saw her again. I miss her, but I liked the new home. There were two humans that I allowed to stay in my new home because I was able to train them to feed me, clean my litter box, let me in and out whenever I wanted, and the house was always warm.

When I took over the home, the male had a sore foot. He broke something. So, I decided I needed to help him at all times. I followed him from room to room to protect him and I still sleep between his legs. The female in the house seemed pretty hardy so I ignored her, but she didn't ignore me. Every day she picked me up and talked to me in a language I didn't understand. I hated it when she held me. So, to show her who the boss is, I sat on her lap whenever she used the machine that she taps with her fingers. I prevent her from using her hands.

Most of all I let them live with me because they are quiet. A couple of times a year I allow them to have a "party", but only because I am able to find a place to hide where no one can find me.

I lived in this house for eleven years and ten of them were perfect. Even though the inhabitants of my house did not go out very much last year, I didn't care. They paid attention to me, petting me, talking to me for some reason, keeping me groomed, and cleaning the house as needed. The cook also tried new recipes a lot and the man always snuck me some of the great tasting food. That wasn't the problem.

What really bothered me was the extremely large noisy vehicles that found our quiet neighborhood. For a year or more these behemoths dug up dirt, cut down trees, removed bushes, and disturbed wild life. Most importantly they scared me. I hated the noise.

It only got worse. Now they are on the land right across the street from my house. First, they took the cows to pasture miles away. Then they dug up the grass and uncovered huge rocks. All day long one of the orange trucks pounded the rocks so hard it shook my house. I was so upset that I hid and only went outside when the machine stopped pounding. Why did they need to do that? I would never allow my housemates to do something like that.

I don't stray far from my house. I miss the sound of the cows mooing with their deep voices. Our neighborhood has more houses now, more traffic, and fewer deer, rabbits, and squirrels. They have hidden also and I can only hope they will return when the orange trucks are gone. Until that day I will stay close to home. The people I allow to live here are so lucky to have me. I let them hold me because I know that they need me to calm their nerves and I am happy to comply as long as they continue to give me my favorite treats.

Figure 9 Illustration Gail Matthews

I Always Wanted to Be a Cowgirl
Gail Matthews

"You're gonna freeze to death, Miss Sadie. Now's the time to come to get you—or it'll be too late. Meteorologists predict catastrophic snowfall and the temperature will drop to at least forty below. That old trailer you live in is gonna be a metal ice tray in a deep freeze. There'll be no help, maybe for weeks. Think Ice Age."

"Thank you, Sheriff, but at ninety-seven, I have weathered many a storm. I'm staying put. You take care." Sadie hung up the phone and looked outside. The barn stood in the distance. She'd secured a rope from her home to the barn. Sadie had learned from experience that it was easy to get confused in a blizzard and this rope was a lifeline.

Sadie made a cup of tea and sat at the table, looking through her box of mementos. There was a plaque commemorating her forty years of teaching. She had no gold watch for service, but her pension had allowed her to follow her post-retirement dream of moving out West. There was the framed newspaper article picturing her proudly holding Lola's reins. What a glorious day. It hadn't started as a shining star. Joe, the mechanic, had delivered the death toll to her old Datsun truck, but a booklet of raffle tickets sitting by his ancient cash register had changed her life. Pictured on the booklet front was Lola, described as a registered seven-year-old black and white quarter horse.

"Hey, Miss Sadie, you wanna buy a raffle ticket? It's for a good cause. Lola's owner, Harvey Hayden, died. You might remember him from his rodeo days. Harvey's folks live back East, and they don't have a place for a colt. They'd like to create a scholarship in Harvey's name with the proceeds." Joe punched the keys on the register. The total cost of repairs popped up in the display.

"Oh, Joe," Sadie chuckled. She swept her arms across her body, "Look at me. My horseback riding days are over. When I was young, I always wanted to be a cowgirl, a cross between Dale Evans and Annie Oakley. I had a horse my senior year of college, but I am well past my sixtieth high school reunion. That's a long time between trail rides."

But as Sadie reached for the door of the service station, a fantasy grew. She saw herself dressed in Western gear: pearl snaps and buckskin chaps. Red, yes, red Western boots. She imagined riding out into the desert and watching the buttes turn to silhouettes against Kodachrome sunsets. She imagined sinking her face into the soft black coat of Lola's neck. Turning, Sadie asked, "How much are those raffle tickets, and how much would you give me for the truck?" It was an easy bargain. Pocketing the tickets, Sadie left improvising a cowgirl swagger.

Sadie examined the article: "The Winning Ticket." Having a horse was more than winning the raffle. Sadie recalled the exhilaration and panic as she held the reins and accepted the congratulatory handshakes.

Joe took one look at Sadie, dancing with excitement. "There's a YeeHAW in there somewhere," he chuckled. "But it looks like you could use a bit of help." Joe, young enough to be the child Sadie never had, borrowed a horse trailer from one of his rodeo pals, and they loaded Lola into it. Joe and his friends took an interest in Sadie and Lola. Sadie's enthusiasm was contagious, as well as the lure of her Southern cooking and hospitality.

Soon the abandoned cinder block building on her lot was converted into a barn with rooms for a stall, feed storage, and tack. Joe and his pals strung fencing, hauled feed and hay, and found, built, or donated feed and water troughs, an old saddle and other tack. Their pièce de résistance was a two-seater surrey. The carriage was in disrepair, but with carpentry, paint, and upholstery, it became a fixture in their small community. Without a truck, Sadie used it to haul groceries and supplies. Children hitched a ride whenever possible. For many years, Sadie and Lola had been invited to take the surrey for a turn around the rodeo arena at opening ceremonies. Joe and his rodeo pals helped Sadie work with Lola, who was easygoing and intelligent. Sadie and Lola also became entertainment for the children at church picnics. Over the past twenty years, she and Lola had learned a few tricks and many life lessons.

Sadie added the framed article, a medicine kit, some country ham biscuits, and a baked sweet potato to the basket she was preparing to take to the barn. The barn was already equipped with emergency supplies, including a mountain of homemade quilts.

Sadie cleared the table by filing the fuel bill, the vet bill, and her medical bills in the accordion folder under "Paid." She put the folder and box of keepsakes in the closet, rinsed the teacup, and placed it in the cupboard. Pleased that all was tidy, she put on her tall muck boots and two thick cable-knit sweaters. Before putting on her heaviest coat, she felt her pants pocket for the Swiss army knife she always carried. Then she tightened the soft fur-lined hood close around her face, moved the basket's handle toward the crook of her arm, and slid her knobby arthritic fingers into thickly lined mittens. When she opened the door, a blast of icy wind and wet snow pushed her back into the trailer. She struggled to pull herself through the door and step into the arctic fury. Bracing against the trailer, Sadie grappled with the ice-encased rope. Almost to her knees, the snow found crevices of vulnerability between the layers of her clothing. She made her way to the barn.

After turning up the kerosene heater and putting her basket within easy reach, Sadie spread two coarse Navajo blankets on the fresh cedar shavings. Leading Lola onto the blankets, she gently touched the back of Lola's left foreleg as their signal for her to lie down. "Lie down now, sweetie." Lola folded her knees underneath her. Sadie encouraged, "Come on now, a little more," as Lola unsteadily tucked her back legs and lowered her hindquarters. "Yes, that's right. I know," Sadie comforted. "I've got those hurtful arthritic joints too." Placing her hands atop Lola's back to steady her balance, Sadie cautiously sank onto the blanket beside Lola. "That was quite a feat for both of us."

Sadie opened the basket and removed their food. Lola moved her muzzle closer to take the offered soft sweet potato and allow Sadie to stroke her arched neck. As Lola's breathing became more laborious, Sadie stroked and scratched, quietly telling the stories of their lives together: the vivid sunrises, the movement of cumulus clouds across the sky, the shape and color of the land as the sun advanced from east to west. She recalled the sounds of children's greetings and laughter at the Sunday picnics, the applause of the rodeo crowd as they circled the arena. Sadie spoke of the love they shared for the rodeo, of Harvey and Joe, and all the people they had met, loved, and who loved them in return. Ears twitching to catch her voice, Lola's sides heaved with each breath.

The kerosene burned low in the heater. Sadie stiffly, sluggishly, pushed herself up to standing. In the low light, she walked to the barn door. She removed the knife from her pocket and forced the door inward. The wall of snow blocking the entire entrance collapsed onto the doorway. She felt for the tethered rope and cut it. Then curling her freezing fingers into her palms, she tucked them under her warm armpits.

A squeal came from the stall. Sadie staggered back to the stall. Lola lay on her side, unresponsive to Sadie's pleadings.

Sadie lowered herself near Lola's head and pulled the basket close so she could reach the prepared syringe. Stroking and speaking the muffled murmurings of love and comfort, she injected the lethal dose into Lola's jugular vein as the vet had taught her.

Settling lengthwise alongside Lola, Sadie listened to the keening wind as the silent blanket of snow fell heavily all about the barn. Sadie whispered into Lola's ear, "Now I lay me down to sleep; I pray the Lord our souls to keep. As we die, lift our souls on high."

Figure 10 Photo Gail Matthews

Pink, The Wonder Dog
Brown Cardwell

My dog died yesterday. Her name was Pink. My dog was very sick. Two Vets checked her to affirm cancer in many organs, starting with the spleen. I do not even know where the spleen is, or what it does. I only know it took my dog from me.

My dog was an AKC registered Petite Great Dane. She was the perfect size for playing doggie games or sleeping with me in my bed.

My dog knew all the doggy tricks of inviting you to play her favorite games: hide and seek, throw the ball–and then look at it from far away (Great Danes are not known for retrieving!)

Most of all I miss her at night. I miss her cuddling with me. I miss her licking my tears when I have a broken heart.

I am now sad and broken–hearted. My family is clearly worried about me. And they should be.

Do I want to go on a great vacation to some fabulous place? No. Do I want a trip to New York to see the shows? No. Do I want a favorite treat for supper? No.

They will all move heaven and earth to see me smile. And yet I cannot. I only want a metaphysical miracle.

For . . . , I only want my dog.

Figure 11 Photo Leilani M. Worrell

Leaving
Leilani M. Worrell

Driving away in the early morning
One last look
My tabby hunches in the window
Not centered, she sits
In the corner nearest me.

I can count her stripes,
Her whiskers hold the dawn.
She sighs, ballooning her fur,
Then shrinks down to original size.

Guilt screams at me across the yard.
Abandoned, lonely, bored:
She pouts.
Then her brother leaps up beside her.

Some Other Words

LOVE

Family, spouse, friends, love endures beyond loss. We are all connected Soul to Soul.

Figure 12 Photo Caryn Moya Block

Fireworks

Gail Matthews

"A friend gave me your number and suggested you might have some insight. I've been dating a man for a while, and I think he will ask me to marry him. I want some clarity. I have been married . . . and divorced."

The psychic asked, "Do you like this man?"

"Yes. My relationship with him is easy. We enjoy time together. I respect him." Shrugging, my face softening into a smile, "He's a good guy."

"But?"

"There're no fireworks. No heat. No butterflies. No weakening in the knees. No sap rising when I'm with him."

"Have you ever had that with someone?"

An enthusiastic, "Yes. It was a grand mal romance, a full-on bodice buster. From the moment I saw him, my whole body responded to him. He was like a drug; I was an addict."

"And how did that turn out for you?"

"He cheated on me with one of my friends. Left me. Broke my bank account and my heart. I was devastated. And yet, I have measured every other man by the strong attraction I felt for him."

Saying those words was a release. Opening my eyes wide, I realized the old relationship had been an addiction—a pheromone heroin-like high creating a delirious delusion. Fireworks are magnificent, but they don't last; they turn to smoke and ash. I had been holding on, craving the high, not the reality.

After a moment of silence, the psychic responded, "This man, the one you are with now; he is a good man. He truly cares about you. He will be loyal and supportive. You can count on him. You can build a life with him."

With new insight, I laughed, "Fireworks are overrated."

Love Haiku
Allita Irby

Infatuation

Is a fleeting thing: but Love

Lasts a good long time.

Figure 13 Photo Les Walters

What's Love Got to Do with It
Nancy J. Rice

The ear, nose and throat doctor's waiting room was small. And full.

A man came out of one of the consulting rooms. His tall spare frame was stooped; there was frailty in his demeanor. His features were still handsome in a craggy way, and he still carried himself with dignity. His clothing suggested vintage prosperity.

Behind him I saw a petite elderly woman I took to be his wife. She carried a heavy woolen overcoat and began helping him into it. Once his arms were in, she had to go up on tip toes to settle it on his broad shoulders. She was a neat and tidy soul with the air of a small bird, rather like a dear little tufted titmouse, quick and alert, flitting about him, keeping an eye out for steps and stages in their expedition.

She spoke to him brightly in a voice she evidently thought he alone could hear. The confines of the little space betrayed her as she said, "Now you'll be able to hear everything I say."

There was a decent pause. Then, almost to himself, he responded in a soft baritone, "Yes, I'm afraid so."

There was love there. Patience. Optimism. Loyalty. All forged over decades, with many a twist and turn. Too much speech and too little were woven into their lives. And they were still walking together, a mated pair.

Soul Friend

Caryn Moya Block

Soul Friend
When I find you in this lifetime,
Like I have many lifetimes before,
Let me recognize how dear you are to me.
Let me hold your hand and support you,
As you have done for me.
Let us dance together through the years.
Knowing our hearts are held safe,
In each other's hands.
For we are connected soul to soul and
Heart to heart for all time.

Figure 14 Photo Caryn Moya Block

The Gift of Presence

Bruce Van Ness

Paul could still feel his wife's presence in the house despite the distance between Heaven and earth. They would always be soulmates whose hearts clasped together as one and whose mosaic of endearing thoughts bound them closer together.

It had been four weeks since Marney passed, just before her favorite season of the year. So egregiously unfair! She had gotten some of the holiday boxes out early in anticipation of the lavish decorating she did every year. Christmas music would sweeten the air with its passion. His step lightened whenever he trespassed into what was a milieu of gingerbread fragrances, yuletide garnish and spirted Noels.

They had gone to the hospital because she complained of left arm pain and indigestion, and twenty minutes later her heart stopped. He was offered the opportunity to peek through the window of the room to see the staff pushing on her chest and doing whatever else they could pull out of their compendium of resuscitative efforts to bring his Marney back. It just produced a ghastly scene in Paul's mind. This surely wasn't the way he wanted to remember her or their last moments together.

Instead, he decided to walk down the hall to tearfully pray and wait for someone to tell him she was better.

Two weeks later he convinced himself to celebrate Christmas the way they always did, by going to the city to bask in all the Yule time bliss, the twinkling trees, the screamingly happy children and the tipsy laughter of spirited adults. The two of them used to stroll hand in hand, sharing whispered tidbits of reminiscences, and spicing it with giggles. Occasionally they stopped in front of a store window and stood like wide-eyed children at the animated displays, then pointing and nudging each other when one of them saw something intriguing down the street.

But today, as he trudged the city sidewalk, snowy drips of sadness continued to splash away the joy and happiness Paul yearned to discover again. He was hoping to find some part of Marney here or at least her essence. Instead faces stared back at him, bland or impatient, or demanding "get out of my way old man." Children screamed they were hungry and parents reminded them that Santa would not come if they didn't behave.

Paul brushed away some of the white flakes covering a bench and plopped down on its cold, wet surface. In his coat pocket he clutched the large golden key Marney had given him one Christmas many years ago. A key that might open castle gates or give entrance to the lifelong journey that was promised during their vows. Inscribed on it were the words, "You set my love free." It was the best gift she ever gave him.

Now when he rolled it around in his fingers, it provided him with strength and a montage of memories that pushed away the tears lingering in his eyes. He could hear Marney's voice asking him one December where should they put the Nativity. "Let's be different this year. Make it a simple Christmas, symbolic of the Christ child's birth."

Then she glided around the room like a sprite flicking her wand, seemingly making the balsam suddenly appear on the mantle, and curl around the railing on the stairs. "There, done," she said. "Do you feel its wafting scent tickle the inside of your nose?"

"I think I do. I think I do," he replied with a smile. Wafting. His wife used words like that. She was an English teacher and reveled in them like a child playing in a pile of leaves.

"Words can give life," he remembered her telling their children. "Hurtful ones can sting for a very long time."

Suddenly Paul didn't feel so bad. Almost joyful. Marney liked that word. He could see and hear clearly now. Strangers were dancing past him carrying brightly colored packages of all shapes and sizes. They shouted Merry Christmas to everyone they saw including Paul. Some of them even nodded knowingly at him as if they knew that his smothering grief had given way to a revived holiday spirit.

A little girl wearing a red coat with a furry white collar came to him and said, "Don't be sad mister. Mommy says Jesus loves you. Here, you can have my candy cane." Then she pranced away with a selfless giggle.

Paul's smile was so big it was practically a grin. He looked at the empty spot next to him on the bench. *"You're sitting right there, aren't you?"*

Figure 15 Photo Les Walters

Family
Bobbie Troy

family is
the fabric
of mankind

the threads
in the cloth
that we weave
together

through generation
after generation
the genes, the tendencies
the attitudes, the religions

too many threads
to name
make us what we are
and who we are

even though
we aren't aware of it

March in March to Dance in April: A Plan to Change

Leilani M. Worrell

My husband never makes New Year's resolutions, but this year he did. He planned to walk every day, even if it was only to the mailbox and back. Our mailbox is in a gang-box at the end of our dead-end street. So, a round trip from our house is about one-third of a mile. I agreed to go with him except if there was snow, ice, rain, mud or extreme cold. He said he would not walk on those days either.

When we had conquered that route without breathing hard, we would expand our walk around the Baptist Community Center, which would add an additional half-mile to our excursion. When we achieved that goal, we would walk uphill to our neighbor's house behind us. By summer, we should improve enough to lose weight.

But then it snowed. And snowed. And SNOWED! When accompanied by the wintry gusts, we didn't walk much that first month. Now you must know that when the weather is simply too cold, my husband will take the dog for long drives. This has greatly helped our mutual retirements; he bonds with the dog while learning different ways of reaching the Blue Ridge Parkway. I have some alone time which I try not to waste but often I do, just decompressing.

I feel guilty for not using this time to increase productivity in some aspect of my life. I searched You Tube for exercise videos and found Marching. Videos utilizing marching as an exercise form are easily available and I could choose traditional marching music or march to my favorite oldies. So in the month of March, I will begin marching while my husband and the dog explore the countryside.

In inclement weather of March, I will march. On pleasant days, we will walk to get the mail, yes, even on Sunday! When April arrives, our new habit will be ingrained and we will continue to walk/march every day.

My birthday comes at the end of April, and on that day we will dance. We will perform the steps we did on our wedding day, the ones we practiced for weeks before our vows. My husband sadly has no sense of rhythm (don't mention this to him. He thinks he does!). So, we had to improvise and we came up with a dance called the Fast Fonzie. You know this dance, although perhaps under a different name. Remember Fonzie from Happy Days and how he danced. He would hold his partner tight and do a 1-2-3 waltz so slowly you would swear the couple hardly moved at all. In our speeded-up version, you hold your partner very tight, close your eyes and feel your partner's heart beating next to yours, and also perform the 1-2-3 waltz step but so much faster than Fonzie. People can actually see you move. As you breathe in the very essence of this person you've chosen to share your life with, you will be intoxicated with love. What an excellent birthday present: I can hardly wait!

Figure 16 Photo Les Walters

Green Friendships
Allita Irby

Friendship like a plant grows.

Like a spring bulb with green shoots

looking for light.

The warmth helps it to grow.

With sun and rain, the plant grows taller

sending the roots out to anchor it.

The Green!

The flower and its parts, once pollinated, will make another plant.

The Green!

The same, yet different.

Oh, but the Green!

Figure 17 Photo Les Walters

Saying Goodbye
Lois Powell

The wind was whipping around our faces. I kept pushing the hair out of my eyes and mouth. He didn't have that problem. His hair was short. The air was chilly and our noses were red. We kept looking at the people around us. Some were rushing to catch their train. Others were running to meet someone while dragging a suitcase on wheels behind them. We kept looking around because we didn't want to look at one another.

Then we heard it. The loud train-whistle telling us it was finally here. Still, we did not speak but we did look at one another. I dropped my head. He put his hand under my chin and lifted my face so he could look at me. I wanted to hide my tears but it was too late. The train stopped behind him and he turned to look at it. Wouldn't you know. It was on time. Suddenly he grabbed me to his chest and we hugged as if we were a dog who refused to give up his bone. I sobbed softly into his chest. He held me tighter.

"All aboard," shouted the ticket man.

My tears turned to hiccups. I couldn't stop the sobs or hiccups. He wiped my tears away with his thumb. He lowered his lips to mine. The kiss was tender yet so moving. I almost couldn't breathe. It was over too soon. We dropped our arms. He bent to grab the handle of his suitcase and moved toward the train. I didn't move. I just watched him go. He lifted his suitcase onto the train.

"I'll miss you more than words can say," I whispered to him. He nodded and waved. I smiled, nodded my head, and waved. Then he was gone . . . back to his wife and family. Me, back to my husband and family.

SORROW

Loss highlights the existence once shared with others. Grief is the path we must follow to honor that loss.

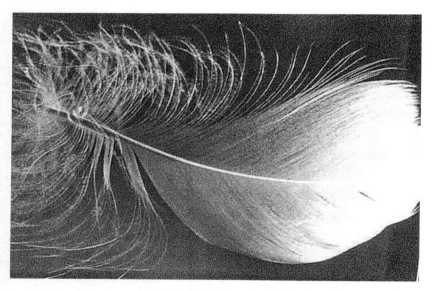

Figure 18 Photo Les Walters

Feathers
Bruce Clark

My daughter's dog, Emma, is a Lab/Huskey mix. Six years old, Em has yet to realize that she is no longer a puppy. Every day, twice a day, we walk, some might say run, two miles. We follow the same path, morning and night, every day, twice a day. We are a fixture in my daughter's neighborhood. Over time the walks blend into one.

Occasionally there is an occurrence. One day while crossing a narrow path, feathers, grey-white, litter the ground. It had the look of a crime scene. From the gathering of the feathers, you could easily see where the poor bird met its fate. Other feathers spread further apart placed by wind and traffic. Em was oblivious to what lay before her. You see, she fancies herself to be a squirrel dog. As such, birds are beneath her and are to be ignored. At the time, my reaction was only slightly stronger than hers. While the story told by the feathers was sad for the bird, its fate was of little consequence to me.

By the following morning, some of the feathers had moved. While you could still see what had occurred, the focus had been lost. By the end of the week, the feathers were gone, all gone to the wind. In the end, the vision disappeared.

My wife Dianne died at 1:05 in the morning. At the time she was in our home, in our bed and in my arms. The cruel illness over which she had no control allowed her one final mercy. She was permitted to die in private surround by our world. She was bathed. I picked a pretty dress to put on her and brushed her hair one final time. Only then were others told what had occurred.

Dianne left our home for the last time early that morning, passing into the darkness, the lady she had always been.

When Dianne was gone, I found myself alone surrounded by our world. I thought I could find comfort there. I thought I could sleep peacefully in the bed where Dianne had died. I quickly learned how wrong I was. Our world had shattered at 1:05 that terrible morning and could never be reassembled. The realization of what needed to be done burned me to my core.

I began in our bathroom. Gone were her toothbrush, her makeup, her lotions. Gone all the items she relied on to begin each day. In the end the only thing remaining to mark her passage, a mirrored tray on which her perfumes still sit. Chanel No. 5 was her favorite.

Our closet, which was always more hers than mine, transformed. Save for a few pieces holding special memories, her clothes passed; some to family and friends, the remainder to charity. The same with her shoes. God, how Dianne loved shoes.

Her dresser was emptied. Gone the silks, the laces, the nightgowns and stockings. Gone the sweaters, the blouses, and accessories. The furniture soon followed. The last piece to leave the house, the mattress on which Dianne died. Gone to be burned, the smoke and ash from that fire rising to the sky. All gone to the wind.

At first the focus had been lost. In the end, the vision disappeared.

Em and I still walk, every day, twice a day. She walks with a joy God has reserved for dogs alone. Every scent a story; every squirrel an adventure. I walk because I have learned that when you're still, the pain increases.

And so, we go, every day, twice a day. We cross that narrow path, every day, twice a day. Each time we do, I remember those feathers and think of the bird which left them.

The First Monday
Allita Irby

It's the first Monday after the service

The first Monday we face without her

The first Monday no hugs for the grandson

The first Monday without her help for breakfast

The first Monday without her taking dad to dialysis

The first Monday we miss her,
But not the last.

Sad News
Allita Irby

Sad news kept me up.

I could not sleep then because

the news was so sad.

The deaths mounted up.

COVID 19 would not die.

Sad news kept me awake.

Sad Dog

Fran Cecere

I was friends with a beautiful woman, Donna, for all of my life. I was with her for every special occasion. We went to grade school together. When we were in our early teens, we met several boys at a church bizarre. She immediately fell in love with Walt. I could not understand the attraction and tried to get her interested in one of the other boys, but she was already hooked on Walt. He was tall, good looking and seemed to be the leader of the four other young men in the group. Soon after graduating from high school, they were married. They had two children. My life path led to college in a different town. We stayed friends but saw each other less often.

One of the times I went to see her, I met their new dog. He was an eight-week-old Beagle. They named him Rascal. He ran from person to person looking for the one who would scratch his belly or throw his ball for him to fetch. He rubbed against Walt's legs and sat by him looking up and whining. Walt occasionally tapped the top of the dog's head, but nothing more.

Over the years Rascal slowed down. He cautiously looked into the room before he entered it. He sat quietly on his bed and didn't run from person to person. He whimpered a little if he had to go outside. No one in the family took him for a walk. I never saw his bowl full of dry food and his water bowl was only half full. He lost weight and developed a limp. His eyes were dull. He particularly avoided Walter.

It occurred to me that Walter may have abused him. My friend avidly denied it. It pained me to see Donna acting the same way the dog did. She never smiled any more. She cooked great tasting food but rarely ate any of it. She pushed the food around her plate and then emptied it into the garbage when dinner was done.

It didn't take me long to realize that Walt did abuse the dog. Donna told me that years ago the dog would rush to Walt as soon as he came home from work. His little tail wagged and he danced on his back legs to get Walt to pay attention to him. It only took one swift kick in the ribs that tossed the dog across the room for him to begin to cower when Walt came home. After a while the dog even shied away from the children. Walt yelled when the kids laughed or made too much noise when they played with the dog.

Rascal looked so sad and lonely. He curled into a ball most of the time and never begged for a belly rub. I tried to pet him when I was there, but he sat on his bed. His eyebrows raised as he looked at me.

It wasn't long before I realized that Donna also changed. She wouldn't go out with our friends. She rarely talked when Walt was in the room. The children spent more time in their room. I begged Donna to see a counselor or a lawyer. She denied having a problem.

Two years later I graduated from college. I went to her house to catch up about how things were going. She finally broke down and said she couldn't stand it anymore. Walt was beating her and she was sure the children were also in danger if Walt lost his temper near them. Within days she talked to a lawyer, got a divorce and Walt took off, never to be heard from again.

A few years later Donna met a great man and married him. They were very happy. The children went to school, got great jobs and got married. Rascal, the dog never recovered. He continued to shy away from men in particular. He never played with the children. His eyes did not regain the shine they once had.

I felt so bad about the situation. The dog was the first sign that something bad was happening in the home. He couldn't talk about it, but he gave clear signals as he tried to protect his family. I will never forget the sad dog that never did anything to deserve the treatment he got. He did not live long after Walt left the house. Maybe he felt that he failed or maybe he just died from lack of love.

Why They Come: Ernesto's Story
Gail Matthews

"Policia! Venga! Venga pronto. Es horrible. Es la casa de mi amigo, Ernesto. Venga inmediatamente, por favor," shouted *Ernesto's terrified neighbor into the telephone.*

Ernesto sat on the cement step outside the local *tienda* of his small village close to the sugar cane fields where he worked. After work, he took his day's pay of one dollar to the store where he bought rice and beans for his evening meal and to have his machete sharpened on the whetstone wheel. Rodolfo, the proprietor, scooped the rice onto a limber banana leaf, folded it into a neat square package, and expertly tore a long thin strip from the side of another leaf to tie the rice package together. He repeated the process with the beans: scoop, fold, tie. "Is Angelo sharpening your machete?"

"Yes."

Rodolfo scribbled the cost on a receipt.

Ernesto thought of his sons. *Where might they be and what has become of them?* "You are lucky to have your son Angelo to help you. Many young boys are not interested in helping their parents. They don't want to do anything, especially if it requires any physical labor," Rodolfo nodded his head in agreement.

"Yes, we have a shortage of labor in the cane fields. The boss is looking into getting machines to cut the cane, but the rough ground would make it difficult, and a machine would cut everything."

"We have seen many changes in our lives and more to come. But for us, life was hard and the work was hard. *Nada fue muy facile.* I am grateful to have my son and my wife. My life is much easier with their help. The other children have moved away. We don't see them so much."

"It is dangerous to travel. Gangs are in the streets of the cities, and robbers often block the roads. Even here, in the country, I worry. And you with the store."

"I worry, but what can I do? I am too old and poor to leave. This is my life. Therefore, I pray *por ayuda de Dios*."

"*Si, yo tambien* with the help of God."

Ernesto and Rodolfo had acted out this ritual almost daily for fifty years. The routine varied only slightly. When there was no work, Rodolfo extended credit to the workers. When they had money, they paid as they could. Sometimes the workers, mostly neighbors, gave Rodolfo and his family eggs, meat from a hunt, and fruits or vegetables from meager gardens.

Ernesto settled his bill with a few pennies remaining.

Today Ernesto wanted to treat himself. He looked over the glass jars of candy and decided on three lemon drops and paid the last of his day's earnings to Rodolfo.

Waiting for Angelo to finish grinding the blade to the keen sharpness needed to slice through the woody stem of the sugar cane, he popped one of the sugar-coated lemon drops into his mouth. At first, it felt rough, prickly, but as his tongue moved over the candy, the bits of sugar melted into a smooth oval. The sharp lemon flavor filling his mouth and nose was pleasing and relaxing. Angelo stopped pressing the pedal that turned the whetstone and tested the blade's sharpness. He took pride in his work and was known to be the best blade sharpener in the area. He smiled as he handed the machete to Ernesto.

"*Gracias, Angelo. Tienes mucho talento.*"

"*Vaya con Dios, Ernesto.*"

Ernesto placed the machete in the homemade sheath, a *vaina*, around his thin waist and walked the three miles home. His home consisted of one room, corrugated tin nailed to a wooden frame and roof. Two windows across from each other and a doorway were covered in strips of plastic that Ernesto had salvaged from the trash at his work. Strips of plastic allowed a breeze to enter and some privacy, although his nearest neighbor was almost a quarter-mile away.

His neighbor had a phone and generously allowed friends to use it. Ernesto had contacted his brother, Miguel, from time to time, and Miguel had called the number when their mother died. Ernesto did not like to take advantage of his neighbor's kindness and offered help in the garden as repayment for using the telephone.

Inside the hut on the dirt floor, a single bed frame was layered with cardboard for a mattress. His clean clothes were neatly folded inside an old five-gallon plastic paint can with a lid. There was an oil lamp and a Bible on a small homemade table. Ernesto had gone to elementary school for four years but, only on the days his father had not needed him to work on the ranch. He couldn't read well, but he liked to look at the pictures, especially the ones of the angels. Sometimes he wondered if all angels were white people with light-colored hair like the ones in the Bible pictures. He had never seen any dark-skinned angels.

Ernesto removed the sheath with the machete and hung it on a nail near the doorway. Then he walked to the back of the hut. The tin roof extended to cover an open patio where Ernesto cooked. He put some wood in the open end of the clay oven and lit it. He would toast tortillas on the grill top when it was hot enough. He poured water from the storage cistern into a pot and added the rice and beans. He placed the pot in the stone fire pit, surrounded the pot with wood, and lit it. Only then did he remove his hat, the long-sleeved work shirt, and knee-high boots. After a day in the sugar cane fields, he was black from the smoke and char. They burned the cane first to remove the leaves and weeds to make harvesting easier. The black on his skin was ribboned with white from his sweating. He sat in a faded green plastic outdoor chair, removed his socks and examined his feet. Ernesto took a small knife he used for cutting fruit from the drawer of a table where he stored his few eating and cooking utensils. With the knife, he cut his toenails and released the ingrown nails from his big toes.

After *cena* (dinner), Ernesto picked up his dishes, the blackened work shirt and walked to the nearby stream where he washed everything, including his clothes and himself. He slipped on a clean, threadbare undershirt and boxer shorts. The hour was not late but the shadows lengthened. He relieved himself before returning to the hut. He spread his wet clothes on low hanging branches of a tree in the yard.

The inside of the hut was cooling down. He lay down in his underwear on the thin covers atop the cardboard. He picked up the two remaining lemon drops and put one in his mouth. Closing his eyes, he enjoyed its tart flavor. Working in the cane fields was not easy. When he and his wife married in their teens, they thought they would have a good life on a ranch, but circumstances changed after a few years and a couple of children. His wife left him for the ranch foreman taking their two sons with her. Ernesto had sold what belongings he had, bought the lot near the cane fields and started another life. He had not seen his wife or his sons since he left. "*Grown men now*," he thought.

Ernesto heard the plastic swish. Sometimes a roaming animal sought shelter so he was startled when he saw a teenage stranger standing inside.

"Who? What?" Ernesto asked as he got up from the bed.

"Shut up, old man. I want your money. I know you got paid today,"

"I have no money," he snapped. "You need to get out of here."

The boy looked around and pulled the machete from its case. Waving it, he stepped back and lunged forward, swinging the machete like one using an ax to chop wood. Whoosh. The machete slashed through the air.

Ernesto raised his arm defensively. Thwack. Crack. His hand and part of his forearm fell to the ground as the blade's tip sliced his chest from throat to waist. Shocked, both of them screamed in terror. Blood. Blood. His blood spurted into his assailant's face, on the tin walls of the hut, on the Bible. Ernesto slumped to the ground, the bed frame scraping his back. Blood spurted from his amputated arm and pooled into the dirt. The boy gagged and turned to escape, his shoes skidding in the blood-soaked earth.

Ernesto raised his good hand to clench weakly below the elbow of the bleeding arm. "*My sons, they will never know* . . . ." He fainted and bled out.

Lieutenant Garcia was sickened at the sight. The inside of the hut seemed to be painted with blood, the floor, the ceiling, the walls, the man. The place reeked of copper, of blood. The incessant hum of engorged flies thrummed in his ears. A lone lemon drop lay in Ernesto's open amputated hand. *Gangs. Looking for money. Looking to earn a rank. Here was a man who had nothing. Killed for nothing.*

Lieutenant Garcia got the number to call the brother Miguel by talking to the neighbor. "Ernesto has been killed. The neighbors want to know if they can destroy the hut to prevent the gangs from taking it over."

"Yes, destroy everything. He'd want that."

"Your brother had very little, but he did have a Bible. Would you like me to send it to you?"

"Bury it with him. His faith gave him comfort."

Afraid of gang violence, no family members attended the funeral. A small cross was placed where the hut had been, and, within a few weeks, the seeds Rodolfo and the neighbors had planted blossomed.

Figure 19 Photo Gail Matthews

Sculpture by Victor Hugo Castaneda
Rancho La Puerta, Mexico

Why They Come: Maria's Story
Gail Matthews

Maria sat on the curb; legs splayed; body bent forward as if she focused on the litter that clogged the drainage grate. A shiny foil from a discarded cigarette pack only purported it to be a sunny day. Maria coughed as smoke filled her lungs. What was that smell? As the baby on her back shifted, she became aware of muffled moans and screams, of the smoke and falling ash. Hell had descended under the guise of an ordinary afternoon. Her mind blocked the assault on her senses.

Alejandro had agreed to take their six-year-old son Dito to and from school that morning. They felt he was still too young to ride alone on the city bus. Usually, Maria placed Carlito, Dito's six-month-old brother, in the backpack carrier and slipped it on to journey across town to the primary school. Today, a cranky, teething Carlito cried for comfort nursing.

Maria grasped and kissed the backside of Dito's hands, enjoying the fragrance of soap and innocence. "Mind your Popi. If Carlito feels better, we'll meet you at the bus stop this afternoon." Maria loved the cherubic feel of her children's hands. She quickly kissed Dito's forehead as he pulled away. Like many children, Dito sometimes protested her holding his hand, but she insisted, "Remember to hold your father's hand. The streets are crowded and the drivers are crazy."

Less than a block away, Maria watched as several delinquents stepped out from the waiting bus crowd and opened fire on the bus. The rhythm of automatic gunfire muted the passengers' screams as bullets pinged against metal and pierced half-closed windows, spilling shattered glass into the street. Then, there was a moment of silence. The automatic weapons' retort stopped. Were the passengers all dead? Squeak. Hiss. The sound of the closed bus door released. One of the gang members tossed a firebomb into the open door, and the shooting started again as the passengers rose from their hovering places to try to control the fire or escape the burning bus.

More firebombs hit the bus. There was no escape from the inferno. Maria watched in despair as she recognized her son's favorite soccer t-shirt. Alejandro pushed Dito, legs first, out of an open window. When Dito tried to turn his head to look backward, Maria thought she saw Alejandro's mouth form the words, "*Look at me. Look at me*," because their son lifted his head toward his father's face. She knew there was no "kind" death in the flames, only torment—no escaping death. Dito's back twisted, jerked and his little legs spasmed as the bullets hit, spraying blood and ripping his body. Alejandro slumped out of the window; the back of his head was a crater of blood, yet he held tight to his son's arms. A firebomb hit Dito's back, rolled and clattered, spreading gasoline along the pavement and under the bus. Hungry flames licked Dito's untied shoelace. Using the tiny body as a ladder, the fire raced upward and climbed onto Alejandro's lifeless body.

The doors of Hell's oven opened. The smell of burning flesh nauseated Maria. The acrid copper of blood. She noticed the sulfurous odor of hair distinguished itself from the toxic gasoline and rubber of the inflamed bus. The crowd backed away as the blast enveloped the bus. The explosion barely registered. Too stunned by the horror, Maria stumbled, her knees buckled. Her body crumpled and folded. She sank to sitting, legs splayed, staring but not seeing the ground beneath her.

Cold Comfort

Gwen Monohan

It's almost spring now,
yet we wrapped ourselves in blankets
when we heard some dreadful news
of one tiny compact car
with super-high speed involved.

How it broke in several pieces
from the force of one huge crash.
And weights of strong young men
sandwiched front and back.

Celebrating once more.
Returning from a basketball game
where their winning team deemed favored.
Drinking to victory again.
Cheering comforts of college life.
It's new-found recklessness and fun.
Life had really just begun
in a novice way.

Now we wonder how it might have been
had this home team fallen short.
Or less of them participated
in racing just for sport.

Had icy beer not been served
in such robust amounts.
Then we pour ourselves another round
as we huddle on the couch.

She: Too Soon to Love Again
Bobbie Troy

I knew her

only twenty-four hours

when she said

I love you

It's too soon, I replied

you're too wrapped up

in loss and anger

to be ready to love again

and a bit of me died

when she walked out

and slammed the door

Domestic Violence
A Two Voice Poem
Gail Matthews

A word	exchanged
A stance	entrenched
A look	leveled
A room	electrified
A step	taken
A slap	landed
A cry	stifled
A blow	unleashed
A scream	smothered
A fury	ignited
A childhood	fractured
A woman	battered
A man	debased
A vow	broken
A covenant	fouled
A spirit	scarred

Figure 20 Illustration Bobbie Troy

Beyond Tomorrow[1]
Bobbie Troy

if I could see
beyond tomorrow
I would collect
my laughter
in a jar
and save it
for the dark days
(you know the ones)

---

[1] Originally published 5/10/16: http://voxpoetica.com/tomorrow-2/

Keeping Busy
Bobbie Troy

playing cards
doing puzzles
visiting friends
keeping busy

doing chores
joining clubs
driving around
keeping busy

eating out
cooking in
seeing family
keeping busy

feeling lonely
feeling sad
feeling old
keeping busy

Figure 21 Illustration Bobbie Troy

The Nursing Home
Bobbie Troy

the old man sat on his chair
hands folded in his lap
eyes staring but fixed on nothing
the teenager who sat next to him
presumably his grand-daughter
sat and cried relentlessly
they did not speak
but if they could
the words would not reach
across the chasm
of what used to be

Figure 22 Illustration Jen Poteet

Hal's Memories
Leilani M. Worrell

Hal lifted himself from the chair by placing both palms on the hand-hewn table and straining upward. His knees cracked like exploding popcorn, and he heard the sympathetic rattle from the aging refrigerator as he glanced around the minute but cozy kitchen. The gleam of the pump handle by the enameled cast-iron sink shot the sunshine into his eyes as he breathed in the aromas of fried ham and eggs. At the rain-spattered window, the curtains tried to be cheery with their printed flowers of red and gold.

"I miss Francena," he sighed, though she had departed over six years ago. He almost saw her washing up the breakfast dishes. The water would have been heated on the wood stove which snuggled like a shadowy toad opposite the table. On that same stove, Francena had often prepared his favorite dessert, custard, made from the milk and eggs provided by their livestock. Her faded yellow cotton apron still hung on a hook near the door. He used it daily when doing the household chores; it comforted him to think she would appear without warning and scold him for doing "woman's work."

He shuffled into the living room and gazed at their wedding portrait, taken over forty years ago. His bride was resplendent in white satin and lace, her simple tiara of interlaced daisies and marigolds, her smile radiant. And comparing himself to the adjacent mirror, he found his cheeks more gaunt, his frame thinner, his then clean-shaven face now brandishing a scraggly mustache, but his steel-gray eyes expressing the same disbelief as today: his astonishment that God had allowed him such a helpmate.

He looked back at the kitchen as the refrigerator gave a last grumble, then fell silent. For a moment, he had thought it was Francena calling to remind him of his outdoor chores. It seemed every little sight or sound reminded him of her. He sighed again and put on his tattered denim jacket and grubby felt hat, then twisted the front doorknob to exit the house. He groaned as he realized he still hadn't repaired that door; it hung askew and needed new hinges. He trod across the porch just wide enough for two rocking chairs, where he and Francena had relaxed after dinner, glorying in the myriad hues of the sunset, its colors more satisfying than firecrackers. Then he turned and looked at the rugged house squatting amidst shrubs that would bloom in spring in yellows, oranges and reds so beloved by his late wife. It had been their shelter from Mother Nature and human storms, and had done a most efficient job. He had erected the structure, but Francena had made the inside a secure refuge.

He trudged toward the farmyard and heard the chickens chattering their hunger. The coop leaned against one side of the barn, framed and wired to repulse predator invasions. He unlatched the gate and scooped up some feed. As he fed his "girls," he clucked quietly to them, and laughed at the way they danced around his feet, stirring up subtle odors of feathers and manure. Exiting the coop, he gazed once again at his home, and pictured Francena standing on the porch, gesturing with her eyes to indicate their hound had been digging in her flower bed again. Her image was so strong and real that he lifted his hat to wave in acknowledgement, then remembered their dog had died over ten years ago. He ran his bruised knuckles through his mostly gone hair and said, "Hal, you must be getting old." That made him laugh, getting old, hell, he had left old behind a long time ago, so now he must be what? Ancient? He chuckled and turned to go into the barn.

The sheltering building oversaw the grassy farmyard with humble steadfastness. Its red paint was weathered and peeling, reflecting Hal's leathery skin and white hair.

The tawny streaks of sunlight gliding onto the straw-covered floor reminded him of his wife's abundant blonde tresses streaked with a few auburn strands when first they met. The Jersey cow lowed at his entry as he snatched the milking stool. He shoved his hands in his pockets to make them less frigid and leaned against the cow's warm belly. The bucket filled, he patted the cow's side and let her out to pasture.

He lugged the milk into the house, and wished his wife were here to fix his favorite dessert. He would try, but knew it just wouldn't be the same.

Some Other Words

FUNNY

Laughter can be found in what we do, what we wear, stories we tell, what we write, and the unexpected punchline. Everyone finds something funny based on their sense of humor.

Figure 23 Photo Leilani M. Worrell

Am I Nuts?

Bruce Van Ness

Am I nuts? I must be. Only my white knuckled hands grasping the sides of the doorway prevent me from tumbling out of the plane. *It's cold up here, and the chute on my back is so uncomfortable. What am I trying to prove anyway? That I can defeat my fear of heights? Does it matter? My heart will stop on the way down and I will never know.*

Are those birds beneath us? My God, I peer upward and try to see Heaven through the white, fluffy mist. *I'm coming Lord, unless you don't want me. In that event I'll be heading in the right direction.*

Are we too close to the ground? How come I can see roofs of buildings, and highways? I will definitely strike the earth before the parachute opens. I'll be a tiny meteorite plunging through the sky. I wonder if I'll make a dent when I hit.

I hear a distant "You can do this." *And feel a hard shove on my back. Oh my God, I thought I emptied my bladder. How come I can see the bottom of the plane? Where's the ground? Did I really decide to end my life on a dare?*

I'm not overweight. How come the rush of the air isn't slowing me down? Maybe I should have grabbed the legs of that bird flapping above me. A duck, isn't it? I swear he's looking down at me and laughing. I want him to be someone's dinner.

My body spins upright. *What a view. Spectacular! I can see for miles. There are more trees than I imagined if that's what those green blotches are, or maybe I'm about to pass out.* "Hey mister! You're not sightseeing." *Am I hearing voices now? Where is that damn cord? Is this . . . Whoosh!* A giant Heimlich maneuver is performed by the cords momentarily yanking me upward, and then giving me my breath back.

My past hasn't spiraled before my eyes yet. Spiraled is probably not a good word to use right now. Does that mean I'm going to live? Is it possible I'm being given a second chance on the roulette wheel of life?

Is that a pond beneath me? And over there, that looks like it could be a sand trap? My God, is that a golf ball coming towards me? Duck! The ground is coming up awfully fast. Gotta relax my legs. They're supposed to be like springs. Uhh. Oh! Damn, that hurts. I didn't know my foot could twist in that direction.

Marinate

Fran Cecere

Every month our writing group chooses two prompts to help stimulate the interest in writing. As soon as I heard the word "Marinate" was the prompt for July, I knew just what I would write. So, I sat right down and started the story. It seemed to form in my mind almost immediately and then I did what I always do. I decided I didn't really know where the story was heading so I shut down my computer and let the story marinate for a little while. I usually like to sleep on the idea and hope that I get a clear vision of a cohesive time line, or at least a believable opening line by the morning.

Two days later I turned on the computer and saw that no new words magically appeared on the page. Maybe I was using the wrong kind of sauce to spice up the story. I gave it another chance to formulate as it marinated.

Four days later, I pulled up the file and stared at the page which still had only the title and "by Fran Cecere" on it. I realized that I was living a lie. I had not written anything. What a bummer that was. So, I got comfortable on the couch and took a nap. I woke up in time to make dinner, clean up the kitchen, wash and dry the dishes and pots and pans, and put them away. Not for one minute did a good story pop into my head while I ate dessert with my husband. However, the ice cream was delicious.

On day sixteen I realized that time was adding up exponentially. Of course, I did not know how to spell exponentially so I had to look it up and that took at least five minutes. I was exhausted after that because you have to know how to spell a word before you find the correct spelling in a dictionary. That's kind of depressing if you think about it, so I elected to just close up the story and get ready for bed.

By June 23 it dawned on me that I might be procrastinating. Did you notice that I used a word pretty close to "marinating"? I was so proud of myself for the rhyming but really was not happy about where the story was going. I really needed to have an epiphany while I slept that night.

July 5 was the day of our writers' meeting. All I had was excuses. This was all I had written. I didn't have a story to read. I thought they would think I was a slacker. This is all I wrote. I confessed to everyone that I did not write anything and hoped they did not think less of me. They thought this was a funny story.

Maybe I should have just said that I was so overwhelmed with all of my other projects that I simply forgot to check out the prompts. Next month I will do better, but for now I really could use a nap.

Figure 24 Photo Gail Matthews

Hair Sanity
Jan Price

Contradiction in hair
Depends on where

In the sink
I don't think

In the mouth
Get it out

Hair on the ear
Cry a tear

On the legs
Matters who says

In our food
So very rude

Some Other Words

Down the drain
Clogs remain

Caught in a zipper
Remove it quicker

Trapped in a door
Hair no more

Tossed about
You'll find out

Flowing down
Beauty abounds

Given away
A thankful day

Curls in a row
Ready to go

Shiny and black
Who wouldn't want that

Short and straight
Always up to date

Making it to the waist
Beauty and grace

Found elsewhere
How dare the hair

In the right place, or out
There is no doubt

Hair is insane
Yet must remain.

Writer's Block
Leilani M. Worrell

Stuck
I am immersed in quicksand

Stuck
Paralysis in every muscle

Stuck
Help?

My muse is on vacation.
I have written 347 opening lines
I have crumpled up half a ream of paper.

My thoughts have trampled
An endless rutted circle in my mind.

Words dance just out of sight
Plots clover-leaf in plaid highways
Characters audition with dueling chainsaws
Hear me! No, hear me!

Evil laughs taunt me as I struggle
To begin to write just one word
Worthy of publishing.

Bitterly I chuckle as I recite
It was a dark and stormy night.
And my muse returns, saying
And then what happened?

Figure 25 Illustration Fran Cecere

Shakespeare Ain't Got Nothing on Me
Fran Cecere

The door slammed and Elise clogged into the room.
"Mom, where's the bug-keeper-offer? She ran to the closet and flotsomed around.

A voice from the other room said, "It's in the thing-a-ma-chest."
"Where, Ma? I can't find it."
"It's near the whatcha-ma-call it."

"Got it. I also need some rubberbanders." Elise squiggled the childproof cap off the can. By that time her mother was standing next to her.

"Don't you dare spray that in here. You will unfragrance my entire housedom. Why do you need that anyway?"

"Tomorrow at school, during lunch, they're having an Olympicnic down near the pond. The Bugs there are dynoskeeters. They're as big as Black Birds. If the bug spray doesn't kill 'em we will shoot them down with the rubber bandits. Want me to bring you one back?"

"No, don't be so flittersome. What would I do with a huge mosquito?"

"You could frame the thing and hang it in my bedroom. It would be my very own "fly waller.
Yes-er-eaty."

Elise stopped playing with the insect sprayer and with real calmessence said, "Oh, Ma, I forgot to tell you, I volunteered you to make your specialism baked mac 'n cheese. It's a real choplicker. The teachers are giving out Gold, Silver, and Bronze medals. You're sure to win the Goldness."

"You're telling me now I need to cook. How much?"

"Just enough for the third grade and the teacher, bout thirty kiddles."

"Elise you have to be just a little more time-ware. I can't do this."

Elise wrapped her arms around her mother's legs and with a sad look that could slushify an iceberg said, "Please, mommy."

The temporary anger the mother felt heliumated away. She turned to the cabinets and started pulling out everything she would need. "Okay, Elise, let's get started with the cooking." She turned and the child was gone. "Elise, Elise? ELISE! The volume and pitch of her voice soared throughout the house causing a vibratingle in the glasses.

"Ok, Mom. I'm here. I was going to do my homework so that I won't fail third grade, but I'll help you instead because the kids would be so disappointed if you didn't make their flavorite meal. You will write me a note, won't you? I sure hope this won't affect your chance to win the first-place medal." Elise sputtered in her most perfect rapidwhine.

The mother looked resignated. "Go do your homework. I'll get this done. I know when I've lost the battle, but I'm going for the Gold."

Love, and I didn't know God had a Sense of Humor

Bruce Van Ness

Some sticky notes I'd like to leave my wife on the bathroom mirror; "I know you're running a little late honey. But don't rush. Promptness isn't your middle name. I'll be waiting for you in the car. If you hear the horn blowing, don't worry, it's just me slumped over the wheel because my sugar dropped, or since it's hot out, maybe the last bit of water has dripped out of my body.

When you eventually leave the house, would you kindly walk over to the driver side first. If you have trouble opening the door completely because of the vines growing over the car, there are some shears hanging up in the garage.

I am aware it's ninety-three degrees out, but you know I don't like to endlessly run the air conditioning while I'm waiting for you because it taxes the engine. So instead, the driver side and passenger side windows will be open so I don't bake too quickly and maybe catch a breeze. If you could just poke your arms through the brambles and prod me to see if you get any moans or groans. And if you're inclined, pull my bottom lip out, and pour one of those little packets of sugar under my tongue. Hopefully I won't be too far gone."

I told my wife I wanted to leave at eight-thirty, although nine was really when I wanted to be pulling out of the driveway. Glad I brought a book with me. At least I'd able to read another chapter before she miraculously appears beside me.

Funny how I used to show up early when we were dating, and Sally would always be ready. But after the wedding, and then with the kids, some freaky, Einsteinium theory of space and time thing happened. I had to wait, sometimes forty-five minutes for everyone to get out to the car. Got so bad, people expected us to be late.

So, what did dear old dad decide to do? Not rush. Lie. Well, just a little white one. Give the family a time we would be leaving, even though it was often an hour earlier than I originally planned. But that backfired, because then I got involved in the game on TV, or doing a small project during that hour, and guess who would be the last one out of the house. Guess who heard, "Dad, you're always late, or Steve, you should set a good example for the kids, and try to be on time."

So now the kids are gone, and I've gotten a little wiser in my old age. I learned from past mistakes. I give Sally a half hour leeway when I tell her what time I want to leave, and that works out better for both of us.

With all this time on my hands, I've also figured out that God is the prankster. We're squeezed down and out when we're born as if in a tube of toothpaste, and then expected to forget about the whole, precious event. I swear I'm claustrophobic because of that whole, harrowing experience.

Anyhow, with God's blessing, we age, and eventually collect Social Security, a relatively recent reward for having survived life's trials and tribulations. There is no security from the aches and pains that come along, and hamper our movements. Can't forget them either, because a year later they're still with us. I feel like the tin man from the Wizard of Oz getting out of bed in the morning. Where's the WD-40?

Another thing, Sally still doesn't like my jokes. Like the other day when I asked her, "If some pet owners look like their dogs, shouldn't some husbands look like their wives?" I mean, who wouldn't think that was funny?

Hmm . . . anyhow, I'm reading a book she left on my pillow. Hint. Hint. Yep. *Marriage Doesn't Have to be a Ball and Chain.* The author's never been married, and he's the expert. Probably has some psychology degree too. Yep. Makes all those analytical types think they're experts on all sorts of relationship problems. Such BS, although I must admit, if you don't say "I do," it does avoid the ball and chain routine.

108

Let's see, chapter fifteen seems relevant since the kids are gone. Empty Nest Syndrome, and How to Prevent Premeditated Murder. Hmm . . . .

Imagine what it will be like when the kids are gone, and they're no longer available to blame for all the dirt tracked into the house. Or you're digging through the refrigerator, and she growls, "The kitchen is my domain. I just want a little time to myself."

"But honey, I work five days a week, and play golf on Saturdays."

"Play on Sunday too!"

So, does it have to be this bad you ask? No, of course not. You're thinking recreational marijuana. Sounds intriguing, but it's not available in all states. You'll move you say? That's not necessary. I'll give you a list of behaviors, and activities you can do together to make life alone with your wife enjoyable again.

"Ha. I like an author with humor."

Oops, here she comes. Close the book quickly and bury it someplace. Don't let her know you're actually reading it. She'll want to lock us in a booby-trapped conversation that might end with her getting out of the car and yelling she doesn't want to go.

Wow, I just realized she's only fifteen minutes late. Gotta love that woman

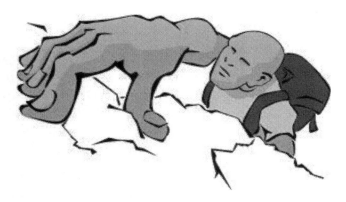

Figure 26 Illustration Leilani M. Worrell

Cousin Vic
Leilani M. Worrell

My Cousin Vic's greatest delight was exploring the Mojave Desert. He never missed a weekend opportunity to take his camper and disappear among the cacti and creosote, accompanied by a nameless girlfriend.

He would regale us with tales of adventures in the unforgiving desert. Sometimes it was the value of a good compass or the eerie howling of the coyotes as they hunted late at night.

He and his girlfriend went rock climbing once in the Joshua Tree National Monument. They spied some rocks while driving a meandering trail through the low hills, and they set up camp at the base.

The dawn found them lacing up their hiking boots and grabbing a water bottle each, ready to tackle the jumble of rocks. Vic scouted the best route to the top. He placed his boot on the closest rock and swung his other boot to the next highest stone. His girlfriend followed using the same footholds.

For nearly an hour they climbed, finding handholds and places to step to gain altitude. The sun had risen, and the day was warm. Vic wiped his bald head with a handkerchief. He looked down at his friend and gave her a wink. She smiled back.

Vic knew they would be on top of the hill in less than ten minutes, so he found another handhold and kept going higher. He swung his arm to gain purchase of an enormous granite boulder as he heard a sound unrecognizable at first. Seconds before his hand grasped the stone, the noise made sense, and he shouted, "Rattlesnake!" Too late, his palm landed on the angry reptile as his girlfriend screamed.

At this point in the story, Vic would always pause and sit back. Sometimes he'd light a cigarette and take a few hearty puffs. But he remained silent, while we were crying, "What happened? Did you get bitten?"

He would look at us as though he had forgotten where he was and who we were. He always blinked several times, then leaned back and slapped his knee, then said, "Well, that was a big old snake, and he didn't like being wakened up that way. Of course, I got bit!"

"But, Cousin Vic," we asked, "What happened to you?"

Vic always said, "Well, I died, of course!"

We heard the words but did not comprehend their meaning for several seconds. Then the laughter and scowls would start. He had done it again! How many times would we fall for the same punchline?

As we grew older, we enjoyed watching the younger cousins listening to the same stories with mouths agape. Knowing all his stories would end with his death, we relished the hush when Vic paused and lit a cigarette before the anguished cries erupted. And we laughed harder than the youngsters, delighting in being entertained once again by Cousin Vic.

Does CPR Work on Electronic Devices?
Fran Cecere

My laptop is old but still very functional. In addition, my hands fit perfectly on its keys and I float on top of them quickly and comfortably. It has all my thoughts, presentations, projects, and most of all, pictures from years ago. We back up our data on an external drive whenever we think about it, but when we're busy, we forget. So why was I drinking a cup of tea in front of something so valuable? Because I was not using my brain that particular morning.

I sipped several times on the hot tea, but then, while looking at the screen, I thought I put the cup down on top of the sand stone coaster, but I missed it. The tittering cup fell onto the table but the liquid spilled onto the computer keyboard, my clothes, and the floor. My scream made my husband run to me, but neither of us knew what to do. I hadn't screamed because the tea burned me. I cried out because I thought I killed my precious computer.

Roy told me to shut it off and I was able to do that. Then he told me to turn it upside down. It wasn't plugged in so I ran with it to the counter away from the wet table, tipped it over, and watched tea poured out. The computer didn't lay flat. It sat like a teepee on the counter.

I panicked, cried, and tried to dry the keys while I used my phone to get help. I googled, "What should I do when I spill liquid on my laptop?" The instruction stated you should turn your computer over. Check. We did that. Use a towel to soak up any liquid. Check. Take out the battery. Roy calmly told me my computer was too old to have a removable battery. While he was checking the bottom of the computer for battery access, I ran to get the hair dryer. With the setting on low, I used it over the inverted keyboard. I was shocked to see how much more liquid spilled out. Google had instructions about drying everything that looked wet. One of the last lines of information said, "Do not use a hair dryer since it heats up quickly and can damage heat sensitive units." Just great! I had not only drowned my precious technical device, but I was now frying it. The last piece of advice on google was to not plug it in for twenty-four hours.

My next futile step was to call the Geek Squad for which we have a contract. Their advice was exactly like google but then the technician stated that the next day we could bring it to Best Buy and possibly they could save the data.

I thought I would not survive those twenty-four hours. I cried, prayed, lost sleep, worried, and essentially felt awful. I grieved everything that was lost. I could replace some of the things, others I could live without, but most importantly, I could not replace the pictures. I ran a list in my head of all the times I used my camera on our vacations. We would probably never revisit some of those places, but I knew I could buy pictures of some of those popular places. Depictions of family events would be lost forever.

So, I spent the night saying the rosary, praying to St. Jude, the patron saint of hopeless cases, and St. Anthony, the patron saint of lost items, and any other saint I could think of and I cried again. I also spent some time thinking about how much a new computer would cost me.

I had to wait until 10 the next morning to even try to turn the computer on. It was torture. At 10 o'clock exactly, I held my breath and plugged in the laptop. The screen almost immediately turned on. As I nervously touched the keys, I watched the screen change as I pointed to the internet icon. Then I checked the pictures, Microsoft Word, and Excel. Everything was there. Again I cried, only this time it was tears of joy. Roy hooked up the external drive and down loaded everything.

I write this today on that very same computer and send a thank you to my husband, google, Geek Squad, and all the Saints who resuscitated my laptop.

Figure 27 Illustration Leilani M. Worrell

Mother
Leilani M. Worrell

This year I have been fooled many times by Mother Nature. She has shown herself to be a trickster utilizing the dregs of her creations. While cruising through the carport I stopped suddenly when confronted by a huge scary bug. I froze, my adrenaline rushing, and the bug stood immobile. We stared each other down until I focused my eyesight and discovered it to be a misshapen leaf. I swear it mimicked an insect in all respects: it was divided into a head, thorax and abdomen with one antenna and five legs, the rest I presumed to be lost in mortal combat. Taking a deep breath to restart my heart I continued my stroll.

Later that same week, while walking down the driveway to retrieve an Amazon order, I jumped to the far side of the asphalt to avoid a dreaded copperhead. Another stare-down, another refocusing and I discerned the snake to be a broken twig covered in orange-red autumn leaves.

A few days later, I walked on our back deck and observed a rabbit sitting near the hammocks in our backyard. I called for our dog, "Look, Sheena, a bunny! Get it! Get it! Come on, you can do it!" Sheena wandered lazily out to stand beside me, looking in the opposite direction from which I was pointing, her usual response. Her head swiveled to face the rabbit, but since it remained still, the dog just looked up at me as if I was suffering another delusional spell. I stared back at the rabbit and yelled at it to hurry, the dog was coming, but it showed no reaction. Stomping towards the still-as-stone critter, I was embarrassed to find only a wind-blown branch from the dogwood tree, its leaflets forming ears and a rump.

This is how I learned Mother Nature has a wicked sense of humor, and I was determined never to be fooled again. But, alas, the best laid plans, etc. The very next day, I saw a dead leaf pretending to be a tattered insect. I reached out to brush it off the poplar tree branch it clung to. At the last second, I hesitated, and counted not three, but seven long appendages on each side, and I squinted to see what I thought were two antennae-like things protruding from one end. I took my phone out of my pocket, opened up a naturalist app and took a picture of the dead leaf. To my shock, the app identified this thing as a "hagmoth" caterpillar who likes to mimic dead leaves, and protects itself by being covered in minute, venom-dispensing barbs.

I backed slowly away, looked skyward, and said, "Well done, Mother Nature, well done."

Figure 28 Illustration Gail Matthews

Flies Flies Dr Seuss Style
Gail Matthews

Flies! Flies! What do we do? I haven't a clue.
They are climbing the wall in the halls. Having a ball.
They're on the floor. Oh! What to do. I haven't a clue.
Flies! Flies! On the screen; I could scream.

Close the screen. Shut the door or there will be MORE.

There are too many. Even one is more than a plenty.

Deal with the ones in the house like you would louse.
Snap 'em. Crack 'em. Crush 'em. Pinch 'em.
That's what you do.
Get a clue!

There will always be one or two. Oh, my what to do?

That's true. But it's easier to deal with one or two.
This is the day. This is the way to stop being prey.
Change your aim. Look at what's really to blame.
Stop the flying vultures; change the culture.

Hercules and a Drinking Buddy in a Bar

Bruce Van Ness

Where to does thou goest oh Hercules?

I goeth over yonder hill to Maid Rowena's hovel.

To her hovel?

Yes, her hovel.

Is this the poor, but beautiful girl who tends sheep in the field?

It is she.

What for does thou goest to Miss Rowena?

I fear love has been trampling upon my heart. I will win her with my muscles.

You believe mighty Hercules that muscles willst make her swoon.

Instinctively I know this to be true.

Your muscles and Maid Rowena at her hovel. Does thou not know she is betrothed to another?

I know not what is betrothed.

Betrothed is to be given in marriage.

Maid Rowena will be betrothed to me. My muscles will weaken her knees.

But Hercules, I mean you no offense, but she has promised to marry another at her hovel in two days and I hear he is a Prince.

She will be wed to a prince at her hovel in two days? Alas, does he not have a princely castle? If no, what kind of noble man is he? I will have the gods send him on a journey to hear his Siren song. Then surely my muscles will impress her.

Oh Hercules, with all due respect, I hasten to say he is a clean smelling fellow.

Is not the scent of vinegar and wild goose lard enough to steal her heart?

To me fair friend, the odor of such oils puckers my nose, and alcohol is the enticement which keeps me here. Willst thou fain to take a bath in heavenly perfumes?

Heavenly perfumes are for slothful and weak, high-pitched men, but to win Maid Rowena's heart, I will surrender my reluctance and dare to wash myself in such essence. Then surely she will catch my scent and swoon at my muscles. Betrothal can only be mine.

Indeed impetuous Hercules, your muscles and lilac fragrance will win her over. Be off with you now to the baths and then to the hovel of Miss Rowena. The gods be with you, and her, he whispered.

What Would You Wear to Go Somewhere?
Leilani M. Worrell

If you had to dress to rhyming success
and your job took you everywhere

Would you wear a ball gown to Churchill Downs
while sporting a Derby hat
Or wear taps on your shoes while spreading the news
that it's all the rage in Ballarat?

Could you shimmy in Bimini
wearing a skirt oh-so-minimi
and limbo all akimbo
to your knees in BVD's?

Would you rather wear a midriff in Cardiff
to do the twist with a corsage on your wrist
Or moonwalk with a Mohawk
While wearing jeans in New Orleans?

Would you wear a feather boa to tour Krakatoa
Or an Easter bonnet with the ribbons upon it
Or very quickly stop dancing the Bunny Hop
If you thought the Rapa Nui saw it?

How about a slicker while singin' in the rain
In Clarksville waiting for the very last train
Could you perform the YMCA every single day
While drinking a martini in only your bikini?

Would you fear getting belted wearing only a belt
On the beltway while singing "I Did It My Way"
Or would it be better to be wearing a sweater
And hot pants while you dance the frug all day?

Would you prefer shaking loosey-goosey to do the watusi
Or do the conga every which way wronga
Wearing an out-of-shape cape made from a drape just to escape
Sporting only a sash for the monster mash?

Could you hula in Hawaii screaming like a banshee
Wearing only a lei and high heels
Or dance the electric slide while watching the tide
In your birthday suit to see how it feels?

Well, this roundelay is getting quite risqué
So I'll leave you with this last thought:
Would you do any of these things
If you were sure you wouldn't get caught?

Figure 29 Photo Les Walters

High Tide
Carolyn Osborne

He sat at the window of the ocean front coffee shop. He'd spent summer at the shore again this year, working as a lifeguard, surfing, swimming, boating, and partying every night, seldom alone in bed. But now the season was changing, parties had stopped, and tomorrow he'd go back to college. Brad's golden summer was almost over. Though he sat by the window, he wasn't watching the ocean view, he was admiring his reflection. He thought he looked natural for beaches—big, tanned, and confident with dense sun-bleached hair.

When a new girl, silvery blonde, walked alone into the shop he eyed her expertly and thought, *this could be almost too easy.* She was young, maybe sixteen. Slender, moon-pale, pretty, and nervous, she seemed a little lost. *Wow. She looks like a poster child for virginity.* She'd be perfect after the easy golden beach girls of July and August. *She'd be a great farewell to summer.*

122

She sat at the little table next to his and soon they started talking. Her name was Dionne and she lived about ten miles away. Her sisters were supposed to take her home but hadn't arrived, and she had no money with her. Brad bought her coffee and told her stories about himself surfing, at the beach, and at college. When he named the beaches he'd surfed, he thought she seemed impressed though she wasn't looking at him. Through the window, she watched the tide come in while she listened, pink lips slightly open in a half-smile, showing the tips of pearly teeth.

She turned to him. "I'm worried. My sisters are very late. Maybe they've forgotten and won't come. I could be stuck here."

Brad seized the opportunity. "Yeah, they probably forgot. My sisters forget everything. It's getting dark. I'll drive you home." She started out saying no, but the third time he offered she accepted. When they left the café, he tried to hold her hand, but she didn't let him.

Seated in his car, repeatedly pushing his hand off her thigh, she directed him along the coastline to an unfamiliar cove. The little cottage there was dark and there were no cars around. Through the trees by the road, he could see waves and the cove's small beach. She said, "They're not back yet, and I don't have a key. Will you stay with me until they get here? I don't want to be out here alone."

"Yeah, sure. I'll wait. This is a great place," he said, "like a private beach."

"Yes. It's quiet here."

Perfect. Anticipation tightened his pants and he shifted in the driver's seat. He reached across to touch her hair, but she pulled away. She smelled clean and nicely mineral, like the ocean at high tide on a sunny day. "You're so beautiful," he said, and he meant it.

She didn't answer. In the moonlight, her eyes glinted like silver, and he felt ready to explode. He said, "Let's not wait in the car."

"You're right. It's a lovely night. Let's go down to the beach."

Perfect. He grabbed his blanket from the back seat.

The tide was in. Little waves gently slapped the sand then pulled back leaving behind them changing runic patterns in the sand that were highlighted by moonlight then obliterated by the next wave. Past the shore stretched the ocean, unimaginably large, deep and dark, unknowable beneath a surface turned silver in the moonlight. He put his arm around her shoulders as they walked, and this time she didn't push him away. When he kissed her, she kissed him back chastely, then smiled.

The sea became flat and still as if waiting for something. He saw that a swell in the water almost near the horizon was moving rapidly toward them, moonlight rolling along it as it moved. "What's that?"

She looked. "Just the tide changing."

She tipped her head teasingly. "Do you think you could love me?"

Oh, baby, could I. "Uh, yes, I will."

"Well, then. Good. Let's go swimming." Her firm voice surprised him.

"I'll get my trunks?" He made the statement into a question.

She smiled again. "No, don't. We have all we need under our clothes."

That's perfect.

They undressed. In the moonlight, her skin and hair gleamed almost silver, nipples like rubies against her pale breasts. He wanted her more than he'd ever wanted anyone. Embarrassed by his excitement, he walked into the water to his waist. Dionne caught up with him easily.

The swell of water was rapidly approaching the shore. Schools of little fish swam ahead of it. Tiny fish bodies gently brushed against their own. Brad usually felt the sea was strange and dangerous at night, but he ignored that in his desire.

Gentle waves and tiny fish washing around them, he put his arms around the Dionne and kissed her again. She wasn't shy anymore. She held him tightly in her arms, their naked bodies pressed together. It felt perfect. For one moment, he wanted never to move again.

But then, he couldn't move at all. He looked down and saw long, thin, muscular tentacles wrapping around him, pulling tight. He couldn't see where they came from. "No!" Heart pounding, he struggled to get free, but the tentacles tightened against his skin. "What is this?"

The dark brown swell of tide had nearly reached them and was flattening out.

Dionne didn't answer his question. She said, "Look. My sisters are here."

Brad gawked as four bone-thin women rose from the swell trailing long tentacled fingers, dripping black seaweed, and smelling like low tide. Panicked, he looked at Dionne and her round, soft brightness had vanished, and she'd become bony, shadowy, and ageless. She grinned at him. Instead of pearls her teeth looked like countless little knife blades.

She loosened her tentacles. With her sisters, razor teeth bared, she pulled him over into the surf.

"What *are* you?" were his last words, then he screamed until he couldn't. It didn't take long.

"What's it to him what we are?" one of the women laughed as they tore and chewed, standing in the water. "You did well, sister. He's very tasty. Perfect." After feeding, they took what remained of Brad with them and rode the just-turned tide out to the open sea.

Some Other Words

PATRIOTIC

Pledge of allegiance, flags flying, rows of white headstones, bugle call of Taps, sacrifices never forgotten, great distances never matter to a patriot's heart.

Figure 30 Illustration Gail Matthews

My Heart
Gail Matthews

My

Baby

Child

Teenager

Adult

Soldier

To Be Green
"que te quiero verde"

Carolyn Osborne

Bullets struck Miguel in his chest, and he went down. Through his shock, he heard his friend Diego say quietly, "He is still alive. We must hide him." Then Paco spoke, "They'll be here soon. Let's be quick and very quiet. We must run."

Together Paco and Diego half-carried half-dragged, Miguel, and he passed out. Next, he heard Paco say, "Be well, my friend. We'll return for you when it's safe." He forced his eyes open and nodded. Over Paco's shoulder he thought he saw a pair of golden eyes peering down from a tree. *Is that a jaguar?* Weak, he dropped his head back on the soft ground. He was well hidden, lying on a bare patch of loam in a cluster of *helechos grandes*, large ferns. Over him stood a big, ancient tree draped with a vanilla orchid vine. Miguel became dizzy and lost consciousness again.

Later he opened his eyes and looked up into the trees around him. They were green and beautiful, the trees of his land. *My mother, my homeland, I'm not sorry to die for you.* The pain was not bad. His blood soaked into the ground beneath him, which made him glad. *I give this to you, my mother.* The gold eyes were still watching, unblinking, and he thought the jaguar would soon come to him and speed his death. *I love my home. I die for my home.* He drifted off into a vague dream.

He awoke to the scent of vanilla. Leaning over him was a slender, green girl: her skin the color and smooth texture of orchid leaves, her eyes the gold of the jaguar's. Her fingernails looked like pale yellow-green petals and her brown hair like tendrils of the vines above them. She had opened Miguel's clothes and looked at his wounds, weeping. As her tears fell on them, the pain in his hip and the hole in his chest stopped whistling with his breath. He reached up, wiped her cheek with one finger and touched it to his tongue. Her tears tasted like blossom nectar. She turned her golden eyes to his face and touched it gently, then leaned forward and kissed his mouth. When the tip of her tongue entered between his lips, he tasted nectar again. He felt a surge of joy and energy, and they kissed again and again. She lay over him, pressing her body tightly against his. She felt cool, smooth, and generous, and it was as if they were becoming one being, their bodies melded together. He felt both serene and excited, and they lay together for uncountable moments. When his time came, his body gave up all it had to her, and he died.

The next day, Paco and Diego returned as soon as they saw the soldiers leave. The fern grove where they had left Miguel was marked around with jaguar prints and covered with a big heavy limb that had broken off the old tree, wrapped in a dense tangle of vanilla vine. The vine's long green leaves were set off everywhere with large, pale blossoms they hadn't noticed the day before. No one answered when they called. "He must be dead under all that weight, all those vines," Paco said, sadly. "I don't think we can get him out."

"I think this is the tomb Miguel would want," Diego answered, kneeling respectfully in the little clearing among ferns and rubber plants. They prayed and said farewell to their friend then walked away grieving while little droplets of nectar dripped on them from the vines above and golden eyes among green leaves watched them go.

"Te Queiro Verde" "que te quiero verde" ('I love/want you green') is from *Romance Sonambulista* by Federico Garcia Lorca

Flags and Trains
Brown Caldwell

The men still march, the women, too
While flags still wave up high
The bands still play and the people cheer—
Except for those who cry.

Then comes a time, when bands are still
And marching songs are lost
Forgotten flags are tucked away—
While all forget their cost.

Yet in time, the flags come out
As newer trains now make the run
The coffins come from far away—
Someone's daughter, someone's son.

Oh, yes, that time will always come
And rarely will the trains be late
They bring our boys and girls back home—
While silently we wait.

Figure 31 Photo Les Walters

Eternal Patrol — An Elegy for Memorial Day, 2022

Gary Misch

We sleep beneath the sea,
Unread last letters home,
Clutched forever
To our hearts,
Though the sea is cold,
Brotherhood,
Keeps us warm,
Don't look for us,
We're out here,
On patrol,
Keeping watch,
Forever.

A Remembrance of the Battle of Midway

Gary Misch

Thunder swept the sea,
The sky rained a nation's feat
Great ships found their graves

Figure 32 Photo Gail Matthews

Concrete
Gwen Monohan

It's been set in stone now.
This life that's passed before
All the uniformed paths
Of one soldier's journey
Have found their moorings.

For the riddle's answer.
Eternal star groups
Laid-up in blocks of
Solid reassurance too.

A place where loved ones
Congregate, aggregate,
Or touch base on their own.
Remembering. Connecting.
Tracing those carved dates.
Or staring at the night sky

As if great distances
Never matter in this
Concrete view of space.
From a war buddy's
perspective.
Just leaning on the rock.

Flagging Memories
Gwen Monohan

Pledges of our allegiance
Or the Star Spangled Banner,
And rising to stand for favorite hymns,
Shared offerings in larger groups
Often remind us, there's
Way more comfort
In those higher numbers.

A caring closeness,
Or shared human bond.
Like the familiar "wave"
At our main football game.
Displaying the team's bright colors.
Often following together chanted antics
Of some costumed mascot.

But let's not forget the unfurled flags
To honor so many brave soldiers
Returned from wars, recent and before.
Plus those small stars and stripes
On Memorial Day graves.
Larger ones too, draping coffins.

Figure 33 Illustration Gail Matthews

Homeward Angels
Gwen Monohan

Frail fronds of low white clover.

Stronger tall sprigs from yarrow.

Plus huge snow-ball bushes

Mounded high as motor homes

Lighten-up our grassy yards.

Cascading celebration.

Some have tiny flowered spikes.

Others, softball-shaped blooms.

Rivaling washed ivory houses,

Shiny as serious metals of honor,
With their milky colored paint.

And when tired soldiers do return
Back to these decorated towns,
We stand, saluting their valued service
Both nearby and well beyond
those rough waves from other lands.

Lacy clean dogwood trees
Lining curvy driveways.
White azalea bushes bright as bone
Highlight greener palettes.
To welcome all fond uniforms
With angel spiral toward home.

Figure 34 Photo Les Walters

They Returned
Fran Cecere

They went to war, a group of friends
Their faces still boyish.
Some returned but they were no longer young.

Others did not return at all.

The neighborhood would never be the same.
Some of their friends did not survive.
Many years later their hair was gray, their faces weathered.
They still talked about the ones who didn't make it.
They never forgot them.

Some Other Words

GROWING - UP

Days of childhood,
new experiences
seeming magical,
learning priorities
and responsibilities
from parents and
other teachers
seldom recognized,
finding oneself,
willingly making
sacrifices, and
accepting growing
old.

Figure 35 Photo Leilani M. Worrell

Bittersweet
Leilani M. Worrell

I missed the school bus that day, and if Mr. Thompson hadn't seen my predicament, none of this would have happened. Some people believe everything occurs for a reason; I don't know, but each of these things led to the next, so perhaps it was meant to be.

The darkened sky threatened rain but despite the gloomy mood, Mr. Thompson smiled broadly as he congratulated me on my perfect test score in his class earlier. "You know, Danny, you are making remarkable progress in Spanish," he said. I felt warmed by both his praise and the car heater, and he laughed as he saw my beaming face. Before we'd even left the parking lot, heavy raindrops began splattering the windshield, making the view shimmer almost to obscurity.

We drove through the new housing development near the junior high school. The streets were absent of the lucky students who had left school on time and were now safely at home. Trusting the wipers to enable our view of the road ahead, we made small talk until a bump and a thump startled us, and panic strangled the conversation. Quickly, Mr. Thompson pulled the car to the side of the road, and we sprang into the deluge to discover what disaster had developed. A mass of something unrecognizable on the pavement behind us made us gasp simultaneously. What had we hit? Certainly not a student; no one had been walking in the rain. We sprinted together towards the lump and Mr. Thompson held me behind him to block my vision of what might have been injured by his driving. When we were nearly on top of the object, it moved and stood, shaking itself free of the rain. It was a dog! Its tangled yellow fur was splotched with mud, and it stared at us curiously, then bolted away and was gone.

"Oh, no," Mr. Thompson moaned. "I wonder how badly it was hurt."

"Well, it couldn't have been too bad; it ran off," I tried to comfort him but I thought I had seen a definite limp when the dog first started to run.

"We should try to find the owner." Mr. Thompson said determinedly as he headed for the nearest house. No one answered his knock. We went to several more doors, but no one knew who might own the dog.

The car now seemed colder than the outdoors since our inquiries had produced no helpful information. There seemed nothing else to do but continue home. Mr. Thompson dropped me at my house and drove slowly away.

Mom greeted me with a hug and said she had been so worried because I was late. I told her about the accident. I had a sudden thought and asked if I could phone some of my fellow students who lived in the housing development to see if they knew who owned the dog.

"I think that's a very good idea," my mother said. "You do that while Lily and I start dinner." Lily, my little sister, began to set the table.

On my third phone call, I reached a classmate who identified the dog's owner as our history teacher, Miss Kincaid. Dreading to inform her, I dialed her number and held my breath. She answered on the second ring. I identified myself, told her what had happened, then asked her about her dog.

"She just ran in not five minutes ago," Miss Kincaid said breathlessly. "I was wondering how she had gotten so wet and muddy! Thanks for your call; I think she'll be fine."

I hung up and took a deep breath. I told my mother what Miss Kincaid had said.

"Mr. Thompson needs to know," I said forcefully. "Do we have his phone number?" "No, I'm sorry," my mother apologized. "Mr. and Mrs. Thompson just got a new phone, and I don't have the number yet." I looked at my shoes, still wet and muddy, and I remembered the dog streaking through the rain.

"Mom," I said forcefully, "I need to let him know the dog is all right. Can I walk down to his house and tell him?" Lily jumped up excitedly and shouted, "I want to go, too!" Mrs. Thompson had been Lily's first teacher three years ago, and they had formed a special bond.

My mother frowned and looked doubtfully at me. I hoped she would see the importance of telling Mr. Thompson this news as soon as possible. She held back the kitchen curtain to see if the rain had let up.

"Well," she said, "all right. But take an umbrella in case it starts raining again." She handed me a flashlight. "Don't dawdle," my mother cautioned, "It will be dark soon." I nodded and we set off

The Thompson's house was nearly a mile away. We had pavement the first hundred feet, then the road turned muddy. Twice Lily almost fell on the slick surface but we slowed down and managed to reach our destination with little delay.

I knocked on their door and the outside light came on. Mrs. Thompson opened the door and exclaimed, "Goodness! What are you two doing out in this weather? Come in!"

She hugged Lily as we entered and Mr. Thompson came into the hall. He was as surprised as his wife to see us. I quickly relayed the good news about the dog, and I saw Mr. Thompson's eyes tear up. He thanked me again and again, shaking both my frozen hands in his large warm ones. Although invited to stay, I explained dinner was waiting for us at home and we left.

The next morning, the phone rang and awakened me. I heard my mother say, "Oh, I'm so sorry but thank you for letting us know."

I shrugged out of my bed, staggered into the kitchen, and sat by my father at the table.

"Who was that on the phone?" I asked.

"Well," Mom began, "that was Mrs. Thompson. She had some very sad news."

I looked up at my mother and tried to guess why there were tear streaks on her face.

"Her husband has been battling a heart condition, and he died in his sleep last night. She wanted to thank you again for making the trip to their house to tell him about the dog's condition. She said he had been very relieved to know the dog was okay. You really set his mind at ease."

I tried to hold back the tears, but I guess I wasn't as grown-up as I thought I was, because I cried right out loud, startling Lily who also began to cry. My father hugged me and my mother kissed me on my forehead, and I knew I had just learned the meaning of bittersweet.

All of Winter in a Night
Gail Matthews

I was born in Charleston, South Carolina. My mother Nobia had terminal breast cancer. When she could no longer take care of a toddler, she asked her sister to take me home with her until she felt better. After my mother died, I continued to live with my Aunt Thelma DeWitt and her family. My early childhood was spent in Pamplico, a small town with less than a thousand residents, located about an hour from Myrtle Beach. Aunt Thelma, her husband James, and their children, Virginia and Joe, who were older than I, lived in a three-bedroom, small one-story Southern bungalow adjacent to Main Street.

On warm and hot evenings, we sat on the front porch in the rocking chairs or the three-seater swing that hung from the rafters. Early evening was when neighbors and children "cut the block," Southern for strolled the sidewalks, stopping to pass the time or the latest news of births, illnesses, and deaths. It was more private than the party-line telephone because anyone on your party-line could listen in on your conversation . . . although impolite, the temptation was known to entice many devoted churchgoers' gossips.

As the evening grew later, swarms of mosquitoes and gnats made the porch too unpleasant. We'd gather in the kitchen to play games and listen to music or programs on the radio. In the summer night's heat, all the windows and the wooden doors were opened. Screens on the windows and the hook and eye latches on the screen doors kept out intruders. There was no air conditioning. The house had an attic fan, and later Joe built a swamp cooler, a system using the evaporation of cooling water and a fan, to cool the back bedroom. Still, often the evenings were insufferably hot, and I would press my body against the cool plaster wall beside my bed or root around in the bed looking for cold spots.

Winters could be mild or sometimes cold enough to create a film of ice in the toilet bowl. Aunt Thelma told us, "Once, the water in the goldfish bowl froze in the living room, and I brought it by the stove to melt the ice." Laughing, Thelma said, "Can you believe it! The freezing and thawing didn't kill the goldfish."

Much of childhood was magical, and every new experience brought a sense of awe. This night was extraordinary, although it didn't start that way. It was just an ordinary Sunday evening in January, and with it had a series of familiar rituals. After supper, the next day's preparations were finalized for school. Papers signed, my third-grade books packed in my satchel, a dress selected with a pair of long pants to wear under the dress because of the cold, and my one pair of polished school shoes—all carried to the room with the woodstove. This was the only room heated in the house except on major occasions— Thanksgiving, Christmas, Easter, a funeral wake, or hosting the preacher for dinner, then the dining room and living room were heated by an oil stove. By 7:30, the family had played several games of *Go Fish* or *Old Maids*. A few families had televisions, but we were not one of them. Sometimes in the evening, we would listen to radio programs or be treated to a reading of *The Bobbsey Twins* or *The Tales of Uncle Remus*. I loved Brer Rabbit, and Thelma was an adept dialect reader.

> *Den Brer Rabbit talk mightly 'umble. "I don't keer w'at you do wid me, Brer Fox," sezee, "so you don't fling me in dat briar-patch. Roas' me, Brer Fox," sezee. "But don't fling me in dat briar-patch," sezee.*

Bedtime was about 8 o'clock on school nights. Sunday was a school night in anticipation of Monday. I changed into my printed flannel pajamas in front of the roaring wood stove, wrapped myself in a blanket heated by the stove, and dashed to the heavily quilted bed. Snuggling between the goose-down quilts, I watched my breath vaporize until I tucked my head under the starched sheets. Soon, I felt smothered and emerged like a whale breaching the surface. Cocooned between the weight of the feather quilts and mattress, it was impossible to move. My body lay molded in place until I surrendered to sleep.

"Wake up! Wake up! You need to wake up!" Aunt Thelma was insistent. "It is a surprise!"

I thought, "Surprise, surprise. It's time to go to school! Yuck! This is a trick." She held out a warmed blanket to ferry me to the wood stove. Complaining at every step, I hurried along, feet too cold to resist.

"It's a surprise. Here are your clothes." Warming by the fire were three pairs of socks, two pairs of jeans, three undershirts, two flannel shirts, a thick sweater, my winter coat, gloves, a pair of mittens to go over the gloves, a scarf to tie a knit beanie to my head, and galoshes.

Then Thelma swung wide the backdoor onto a wonderland of white. Glistening from the back porch light and the distant streetlights, snowflakes whirled and danced beneath their globes like a gazillion fireflies.

I stood mesmerized. The sight and the cold took my breath away until I heard the voice of my best friend, Bob Calcutt, yelling. He and his two brothers, Ben and Steve, had already started a snowball fight. We met in the Cusack's side yard, frolicking and laughing. Bob molded a small soft-packed ball of snow on his gloved hand and threw it, landing right between my eyes. This was the challenge, the gauntlet tossed. Through good-natured heckling, "You can't hit me" or "Missed me!" We chose sides, two against two. A direct hit was an excuse to fall, giggling, onto the snow. We battling daredevils moved to swing our arms and legs in wide arcs to create angel patterns in the heavenly white.

Aunt Thelma appeared with two well-seasoned cookie sheets and a roll of wax paper. She led us to the hill near the church. We rubbed the wax paper on the bottom of the pans. Sledding. What could be more exciting than a sled ride of four or five feet! We pushed off and raced, hearts pounding and smiles frozen on our faces.

Another neighbor who saw us on the church footpath brought over mugs of hot chocolate, marshmallows bobbed like corks from the steam. Homemade of Hershey chocolate powder, granulated sugar, boiled whole milk with an added touch of vanilla and cinnamon, the concoction warmed our bodies from stomach to fingertips and toes. Energy renewed; we were ready for a new adventure.

Mrs. Calcutt, the boys' mom, sent us on a scavenger hunt for fresh snow. We scraped it from the hoods and tops of cars parked along the street. In small bowls, she turned it into snow cream! She poured the thick, sweet condensed milk and fragrant vanilla over the clean snow—Ambrosia of the northern gods.

The snow clouds moved away. The night sky was clear, the moon and stars shining brightly.

Not yet ready to end the evening, Ben yelled, "Let's build a SNOWMAN!" Scraping the fleeting snow from the surroundings, our construction had almost as much crushed grass and crumbling leaves as snow. He was all of twelve inches tall, or maybe less. The carrot nose looked bigger than the snowman. A single sock became a scarf, a jar lid, a hat. Pebble eyes and mouth defined our creation.

We were exhausted and returned to our respective homes to rest in our feather cocoons. My chapped, red face rubbed against the stiffly starched pillowcase. I cushioned my hand between my cheek to prevent chafing. Was this a dream? The next morning, the only evidence of our extraordinary night lay in the small melting snowman. All other traces of its magic had vanished except in my memory and my heart.

"If you do not enjoy a moment, you lose it forever. If you enjoy it, it is yours forever." — Debasish Mridha

Figure 36 Photo Les Walters

An Afternoon Dream
Gary Misch

I close my eyes,
Eight bells sound,
"Relieve the watch
Relieve the wheel
And the lookout."
My ears perceive the prow
As it cuts the waves,
Splicing the seas,
Throwing the waters aside
With that powerful hiss.
My nose wishes it could smell
The oils that keep
This steel engine whole
In the face of sea and salt,

151

I don't want to open my eyes.
When I do, I shall be
An old man again,
Sitting at my desk,
In my house,
In the forest,
Far from the sea,
While young men do the work,
I long to do.

On Aging
Allita Irby

I never thought I would
choose fresh fruit and yogurt
over bacon and eggs for breakfast.

I never thought I would
Choose Saturday night "in" vs. Saturday nights "out."

I'm older. I'm wiser,
But still young at heart.

Figure 37 Photo Fran Cecere

May I?
Gwen Monohan

The Salesman said:

"So may I interest you
in a brand-new pick-up truck?
It's yellow and blue,
shiny through and through.
With wide-set tires
to handle some serious mud."

"I'll bet your son would be
more than thrilled
to take it for a test run."
Then Mom turned the key
to fire-up a small battery.
And her bouncing toddler
was soon rolling away.

Tik Tok vs. Tic Tac Toe
Allita Irby

Tik Tok, Tik Tok, Play.

Games keep boredom at bay.

Tik Tok, Tik Tok, Play.

Tic Tac Toe, Tick Tock.

Tic Tac Toe, Tick Tock.

Figure 38 Photo Les Walters

Dance Ballerina Dance
Rose Lyn Jacob

Parents almost always have ambitions for their children. It can't be helped, it has something to do with not realizing their own ambitions or dreams. I am a victim of a mother's ambition. Oh, to be sure, there was pride in my graduating from high school, college, and graduate school, but, to her everlasting disappointment, I did NOT realize her one true dream. I did NOT become a ballerina.

On my bedroom wall hung a black-framed painting of a ballerina. It appeared the summer my parents moved into a new house while I was away. My new bedroom was done in a very girly HOT PINK and WHITE. The walls were WALLPAPERED white, not painted. The border at the top was a ring of pink, flocked curli-cues. The carpet matched the electric pink flocking. The bathroom had hot pink towels and a vanity chair with a hot pink cushion. Please note that I had specifically told my mother

156

that I wanted my new bedroom to be blue and green. At night, when the light switch flipped, the hot pink of the walls and carpeting continued to vibrate for several moments before plunging into darkness. My mother had given me HER dream room.

For me the pink brought back painful and humiliating childhood memories of pink leotards, tutus and dance class. As one verse from *A Chorus Line* recounts, "Up a steep and narrow staircase, to a voice like a metronome." Oh, I remember the steep and narrow stairs to the third-floor studio. How my mother ever made it up those stairs, week after week, wearing a full girdle and high heels I don't know. I also WILL NEVER KNOW how she stuffed me, like a little sausage, into my leotard. It is a mystery, but she was nothing if not determined.

Until the ordeal of ballet lessons began, all I knew about dance was what I learned square dancing in gym class. I liked it very much although I DID have a hard time knowing which direction to doe-see-do and frequently got "to the right" and "to the left" confused.

But ballet dancing was different. Mostly it was different in that there was no actual dancing involved . . . just endless exercises to make us graceful, flexible, and strong. All practices were performed in front of floor-to-ceiling walls of unforgiving mirrors.

Our teachers were a married couple, Madame et Monsieur Paquot. She was French and he was Russian. Both were adept with the long, wooden pointer that pushed our feet into one of five positions, lifted our arms, adjusted our hands, or raised our chins. They also poked derrieres which needed to be tucked in or backs that needed to be straightened. I suspect back in Russia and France, the stick was applied with a bit more force.

Each lesson concluded with the same ritual. After an hour of repetitive torture, foot smacking, and exacting instructions in either Russian or French, we had one moment of individuality. This was a chance to exhibit our grace and bearing. I lined up with the other girls, each waiting for a pause in the music from the piano. We each took our turn alone to walk across the diagonal of the room with our arms lifted elegantly and fingers delicately curved, with stretched necks and straight backs. With pointed toe and slight elevation, we walked gracefully to one of the Paquots, who held a basket of chocolates. A pause, a curtsey, and then, finally, a reward for our efforts: one chocolate popped into our mouths. Another curtsey, a Merci Madame or Merci Monsieur, and back on our toes until we reached the back walls.

No, those years at the dance studio did not make me into a dancer or a ballerina, but it made my mother happy, if somewhat delusional about my abilities. That was the closest she got to living out her fantasy and ambition through her child. She wasn't the first mother, and she probably won't be the last to have her dreams dashed, but I really enjoyed the chocolate.

Growing Up is Difficult
Lois Powell

Chris sat on the brick patio in a black wrought iron chair. The wind ruffled his sandy-colored hair that fell straight to his ears with a fringed bang. His freckled face was slim and long. His nose was straight and his mouth was pouting. He slumped in the chair. He stared at the can he held in his hand. He turned and looked at his mom sitting next to him. Next to her sat his grandfather in a wheelchair. Diagonally across from him was his brother Jeff who was nine years old. There was no conversation going on between the mom and the grandfather. They just sat there. Mom placed her hand on the grandfather's hand. He didn't react. He didn't move his head to look at her. It was as if he had no feeling in his hand. Chris stared at the other people on the patio, his eyes following the people in wheelchairs. He watched a woman with a walker.

Jeff suddenly jumped up pointing to something on the ground.

"Wow! Look at that bug, Chris," Jeff said.

Chris got up to follow his brother. His black short-sleeved T-shirt was long over his baggy jeans. Written on his shirt in brown letters was, "Way to Go!" The clothes looked too big for his body. His sneakers were dark brown with a beige stripe design on the side. He was not quite five feet tall. He started hopping from brick to brick like hopscotch, following the bug. He stopped and looked around, seemingly bored. Throwing the soda can on the ground, he crushed it, picked it up, and threw it in the trash can next to him. Jeff ran back to his chair and sat down. Chris crept up behind him and started tickling him and messing up his hair.

Finally, Mom stood up, kissed grandfather on the forehead, walked across the patio, and opened the gate to leave. Chris saw her leaving. He ran and jumped over the three-foot wall around the patio. He dashed toward a blue Chrysler SUV in the parking lot. Neither he nor Jeff said goodbye to their grandfather.

CHRIS'S INNER MONOLOGUE

Why does Mom make me come to this nursing home to see Grandpa? There's nothing to do except sit around and watch all these old people. Most of them can't walk. Gosh! That old man can't even wheel himself with his feet like the others do. He has to have somebody push him. Who wants to be here? I could be home hangin' with my friends. I could be practicing my soccer or playing games on my computer, or playing with Blacky. I love that dog. He's so fun. The best Frisbee catcher around.

Geez! Mom just sits there next to Grandpa but that's not my Grandpa. My Grandpa used to take me fishing. He taught me how to bait my hook. We'd laugh and talk and fish. We'd leave early in the morning, just me and him. It was the best. Now he don't say nothin'. That's not my Grandpa who took me to the train store and looked for the right pieces to add to his cool train set. Boy, that train setup was awesome. We'd play for hours. Grandma would yell down the basement and ask, "What on earth are you two doing down there?" We'd just laugh. Even Jeff, who a pain sometimes, would be there and it was okay.

I hate being around these old people. Why'd Grandpa have to get old? Some of my friend's Grandpas still played with them and they're old. Why can't my Grandpa still play with me? Why'd he have to get sick? The whole thing stinks. I won't be like these oldies when I get old. I won't just sit around in a wheelchair or walk with one of those things with wheels. No Way! It ain't gonna happen to me. Might as well look at this stupid bug. Boring! Guess I'll toss this can. Bugging Jeff is a good idea. Gives me something to do.

Yea! Mom's leaving – finally. I'm outta here.

Figure 39 Photo Fran Cecere

Cabbage Patch Kids
Gwen Monohan

We heard it once rumored in the past,
though this advice didn't last,
that babies were found
in cabbage patches.
Was it because this round plant
is referred to as a head?
Or perhaps it alludes to
any flowering growth instead.
Or just the hidden labor
of the birthing process,
parents didn't want discussed.

And doesn't the mysterious process
of human reproduction continue
even after gaining knowledge?
We study our miracle infants
at birth and long beyond.
Wondering at the joy
of every simple playful gesture.
Each fun game of rag doll, peek-a-boo,
or garden hide and seek.

Green With Envy
Allita Irby

When I was 18, I saw him walking on campus

beside the Student Union building.

When I was 19, we were going steady.

When I was 20, I saw him holding hands with Hela Tramel and

walking on campus

beside the Student Union building.

Then I wanted him back.

When I was 21, I announced my engagement to someone else.

Then I was GREEN no more.

Figure 40 Illustration Fran Cecere

Dance

Fran Cecere

My parents owned a family restaurant from before I was born until after I finished college. I remember all of the holiday memories there. I learned to greet strangers, throw parties, make change when customers paid their checks, and how to add, subtract, multiply, and divide. All of that is pretty normal for a restaurant. What isn't normal is that I learned to dance there.

I was about ten and in constant movement. When the music was playing on the juke box, I would sing or move to the beat. There was a gentleman named Lyman who came to the bar every evening after work. He was so tall. I remember thinking he was a gentle giant. One day he talked to my mother and asked if he could teach me to dance.

We had a large dining room which was used mostly for lunch and supper diners, but also for large parties that were occasionally scheduled. There was a small dance floor and a Juke Box in that room also. Lyman asked me if I would like to dance. I had never danced with anyone. He put some coins in the record player and selected several slow songs. He proceeded to slowly guide me across the floor, making me keep my head up instead of looking at my feet.

Once a week for three weeks we danced and I felt that he was the most talented person I have ever met. I later asked my mother if I could take dancing lessons and she enrolled me in tap classes. I kept at this for about two years and each lesson I thought of Lyman and wondered if he could tap dance.

I remembered everything he taught me and all my life I was able to follow the steps of any person who asked me to dance. It even helped me with the polka which was a popular song at weddings and parties. When swing dancing became popular, all I needed was a talented partner.

I loved to dance and followed the latest fads. My friends and I especially loved the twist. With a quarter we could play three records and dance in the empty dining room.

You never know when a teacher is going to affect the rest of your life. Lyman remained a friend to my parents and my favorite teacher. When I got older, I got a chance to thank him. I wish I could dance with him one more time.

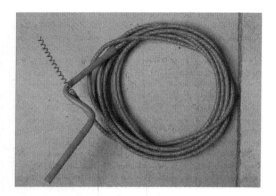

Figure 41 Photo Gail Matthews

The Snake of Eden
Gail Matthews

The oversized SUV sped up the driveway. Gravel ricocheted off the siding. A whirl of autumn leaves sought safety at the base of the fence posts lining the driveway. Seated in the kitchen, Mom watched through the glass storm door. The car overshot the parking area. There was a squeal from brake pads and a ratcheting of the emergency brake. The car stopped just short of the magnolia tree.

Helen wrenched the car door open. The contents of her purse tumbled onto the grass. Mindless of the destruction, Helen stomped on her cosmetic bag. *Crunch.* Glass broke. She didn't stop. With piston pace, she crossed the yard. Helen jerked open the glass door; it withstood the storm. "MOM!"

Mom looked at the small dot tattoo, just a point in her palm, before she moved to embrace her daughter. Hot tears ran down Helen's splotched face. Her wrath turned into hiccupped sobs. With tender care, her mother guided her to a chair, brought her daughter a cup of water, and settled in to listen.

"You don't understand, Mom. I was right. John simply will not admit that I was right. He's a bully. Always attacking. Telling me I don't know what I'm talking about. He says,

166

'Honey, you just don't understand how this works.' I hate it. He's so patronizing." Helen slapped the cup on the table, splashing water.

"Do you love him?" Mom looked straight at her daughter.

Helen glared back. "What's love got to do with it? Love!" She sneered and crossed her arms in defiance. "I'm not so sure at this moment."

Mom looked down at her opened palm and remembered why she'd gotten the dot tattoo meaning "you may have a point". The phrase had saved her from many confrontations. Considering what to say, she walked over to the sink and began to load the dishwasher.

"Last week, the dishwasher began leaking around the bottom of the door. I thought there was trash in the trap, so I emptied the dishes, took the top off the trap and cleaned it. But when I started the dishwasher, it still leaked. Since that didn't work, I removed the entire trap. I took out pieces of glass and several thick wads of gunk. When I started the dishwasher, it still leaked. I suggested we call a plumber, but your dad was adamant. 'No,' he said, 'The last time we called a plumber, it was over $200. Paid two men to do the job of one. All the helper did was bring the drain snake on the porch and watch the plumber inch it down the drain. If we're going to spend $200, let's just buy a new dishwasher. That one must be at least 20 years old.' "Not yet. I said to your father. Let me look online and see what else causes a dishwasher to leak around the door. 'Honey, don't waste your time. I'll get a snake. That'll fix it,' he said."

"Why doesn't Dad ever look anything up online?"

"Likely the same reason my father wouldn't stop to ask directions," Mom said.

"The dangly bits get in the way." Helen watched her mom's eyes roll skyward at her comment. Distracted by watching her mother rearrange glassware to get the last dish on the top rack, Helen's temper cooled. "Give it up, Mom. That bowl is not going to fit."

"Right. Seed for the next load." Her mother said as she placed the bowl back in the sink.

Helen glanced at the dishwasher. "That's not a new dishwasher, so . . .?"

"I searched online," replied Mom. "Several sites suggested it could be a brittle or cracked rubber gasket. Time for another plan.

"Let's go to Lowes. Buy a new gasket. And we'll look at new dishwashers, I said to your father. 'And, I'll buy a drain snake,' he said. You can't put a snake in the dishwasher drain, I cautioned. 'I'll put it in the same place the $200 plumber did. I'm telling you; a snake'll fix it.'

"Lowes didn't stock the gaskets. The salesman told me I'd need the model number to order the seal online. We looked at new dishwashers. Your dad bought the longest snake in the store.

"When we got home, I skimmed through twenty years of appliance manuals and registrations while your dad inched down a snake long enough to reach the next state. 'The snake didn't meet any resistance. Came out clean. It's fixed,' he said. "I found the original dishwasher manual and invoice. I reported." 'Packrat,' he teased."

"Your dad grinned when I called him 'snake charmer.' Gave me a hug and strutted off to the gym with the stride of the confident hero, totally satisfied that the snake fixed it. But when I turned on the dishwasher, water gushed out. Time to order a new seal. On the order site, was a video link to *How to Install a Gasket*. Another video link was entitled *I Failed Twice*. That looked like my story. I'd found Plan Three.

"I mixed baking soda with a little water and poured it down the dishwasher drain followed by a cup of white vinegar. Waited 10 minutes. Poured a kettle of hot water on the action bubbling in the drain. A moan, 'ooooaaaah.' A bellow like an ancient door opening in a horror movie came from the pipes. I poured another kettle of hot water. I tested the dishwasher. Dry floor. Success!"

Helen laughed as her mom waved her hands over her head and swayed, a seated version of her happy dance.

"When Dad came home and heard the dishwasher running, his smile lit up his whole face. I love his smile. 'Look at the money I saved. See, I told you the snake would fix it.' Maybe it was a combination of things, I suggested. 'Nope. It was the snake. Told you the snake would do it.' You're my handyman," I said to your father.

"But, Mom, *you fixed it*." Helen shook her head. "He should have known better. He is sooo not a handyman."

"True." Mom nodded.

"Did you tell him?"

"No. That was my first divorce and maybe my second. For husband number one, I could spit out, 'I'm right.' with red hot righteous indignation. It's a wonder the words didn't singe my throat. Husband number two, my line was much cooler, 'You know you're right, but I think you're wrong,' then I'd smugly walk away. You can know you are right and not make another person wrong. Save the fight for the big stuff."

"I don't agree. I'm important too and I deserve respect," said Helen, indignation rising in her voice.

"I agree." Mom looked at her hands in her lap, fingers locked and palms up. She looked at the small, tattooed dot, a simple reminder. A faint smile softened her face. "You may have a point, dear."

She wondered when her daughter would be ready for her tattoo. Maybe a bigger dot.

Figure 42 Photo Les Walters

Bumper Blues

Gwen Monohan

I learned to drive in West Virginia on hills and curvy roads. Mostly my dad helped me get started because our school didn't have driver's education at that time. However, unless we were in a huge parking lot, nearly empty, Dad got kind of nervous before long and suggested we try again at a later time. Since he had already had a heart condition when I was sixteen, I didn't argue.

My brothers and I learned to drive first with his Volkswagen. Dad was thrilled to have a little car that didn't use much gas and I thought it was neat that when you did run out (which I did) there was always the reserve tank with more than enough to make it to a station. Plus, it was fun learning to shift gears in the little bug.

I remember having two sort-of wrecks back then. One was when I backed into a taut supporting wire from a telephone pole that I saw too late. That one didn't seem to do much damage since I wasn't going fast. No one in the family even noticed it for a couple of days where a slight ridge marked the rear bumper like a thin stripe. My later wreck caused more changes to the front end.

I was returning from a high school basketball game and had to take some friends home by going over a series of railroad tracks. The warning lights weren't blinking yet, but I remembered to stop and look both ways for a possible train anyway. And there was one. I could see its bright beacon in the distance, so I stopped. After a minute or so we noticed the train was only moving very slowly, so my riders all advised me to gun-it on across. I began to ease forward while all the time watching in case the train began to speed up. In fact, I watched the train so closely that I drove right off the road in that direction, onto and over the main track on the train side and there we were stuck. I watched the engine still approaching slowly and the light appeared bigger.

Everyone was yelling and laughing and telling me to blow my horn to warn the train of its impending danger. I finally did have the thought that getting out of the car might be a good idea, so I told everyone to vacate the Volkswagen, all four of my passengers. We had three kids crammed in the back. It took nearly a minute to do and this was before seat belts.

By that time someone who was lined up behind me to cross the tracks got a chain from his truck. He pulled around in front of me and attached the chain to my front bumper. Then he gradually hauled us back on the roadway. By that time the train engine had stopped until we all cleared the area.

Now the front bumper had a wound like a big upside-down U. However, all my passengers said that it was their most exciting ride yet. But being the driver, I felt more relief than anything when we were on the road again. My long-suffering parents were just relieved that no one was hurt.

Viv and the Fools of April
Carolyn Osborne

It's April first. I turn nineteen. I cut Sociology and drive into the mountains. It's a beautiful morning. The back roads are blessedly empty, and Ringo, my leaf-green Honda, my graduation gift, skimmed across the rutted gravel.

I'm driving too fast. I can almost hear father saying, "Slow down, Aviva. The road will wait for you." I wish he'd call me Viv. Aviva means "blossoming" but it's an old name—like someone's great-aunt. I'm no old Aviva. I'm Viv. It's spring, I'm nineteen, and life is good.

My new boyfriend Larry is taking me to a fancy restaurant tonight for my birthday. There'll be French food, no doubt lots of wine, and after that, who knows? Maybe this'll become my first overnight date. I think I'm ready for one of those. Larry's cute and such a good guy. He's even in the Jewish fraternity. I think Mom would be pleased if we became—something. I should look extra good tonight.

My mind's busy, I'm not paying attention, and gravel roads are tricky. When I take a curve too fast, we skid out, almost going over the side. I turn Ringo off and stop to breathe. Then I start up more carefully, scolding myself. *I can't afford to be reckless. I'm a grown-up now. I know that what Dad calls the stakes of failure get higher every year.*

So, I drive more carefully. That's a good thing. Several times young squirrels race into the road, almost under my wheels. I swerve to avoid hitting them. *Stupid squirrels. Last week one of my classmates joked about "suicide squirrels of March." I wondered what he meant but get it now.*

Suddenly, a bump. Worried that I'd hit one, I look in the rearview mirror. Something lumpy and dark is on the road behind me. My heart starts pounding. *What if it's still alive, poor thing?* I find a wide enough place to make a U turn and go back, but it's just a chunk of bark.

There are more crazy critters ahead where the land's been cleared, little rabbits hop onto the road. Stupid rabbits. *Maybe "madder than a March hare" means something. How can these creatures be so unaware?*

I turn on the radio. Every single song is about love—love won, love lost, or love longed for. I change channels and let Grieg's Piano Concertos ease me into Charlottesville.

To get to my apartment I must negotiate the notorious "corner" at Elliewood Avenue. That's difficult driving any time. On a spring day, it's almost impossible. Students are everywhere: in the road, ignoring cars, blocking traffic, taking their time, caught up in themselves or each other. They're not even thinking about being careful. I decide they're mostly thinking about sex. *Stupid, careless students.*

Getting ready for my date, I slip a toothbrush, my pills and spare panties into my bag. Then I stop and wonder—*am I just another April fool? It could be I am. Stupid me.*

Figure 43 Illustration Leilani M Worrell

Eight Hundred Miles a Week - Or How I got my College Degree in California
Leilani M. Worrell

The asphalt tapeworm
feeds on his tires so
sometimes he needs new shoes;
desert dust storms have pitted
his windshield which
kamikaze insects find irresistible,
like sailors lured to a rocky death by sirens.

I fill his belly with liquid fire
and together we journey
across sandy plains,
through creosote forests.
We wind through the Tehachapis
like a blind snake,
following a scent trail of semis,
squirting into the interstices of traffic,
and dodging the Man What Am.

He likes schussing down the hillsides
almost as much as he revels
in his fuel-injected power
to out climb the big boys.

174

We are bored in the heartland,
our path straight as a starched parson
and bordered by green and brown,
the coming crops and the fallow fields.

Arrival, and we circle the lot like land sharks
desperate to join in the parking frenzy:
the winner gets the closest shade.
Patiently, he naps while I study,
his dreams crowded with shiny waxy pampering,
serpentine oxbows of tarmac
and checkered flags,
while I glean the jetsam
showered on the acolytes
by the old men of the See.

Eight hundred miles a week,
I pilot my craft
to learn my craft.

Figure 44 Photo Caryn Moya Block

She Sleeps
Caryn Moya Block

She sleeps
Unlimited possibilities
Wrapped up in the
physical body of a
Little girl.

The Universe waits
to see what choices
she will make
What lives she will touch
and how much Love
she will bring
to her world.

A divine spark
A galaxy in the
universe of
infinity
She sleeps.

Allie and Ted

Carolyn Osborne

"Mommy, I'm gonna marry Ted, you know." Mommy looked up from the lunches she was packing and smiled. "Is that right, Allie?"

"It is, an he's gonna go to work and, and I'm gonna stay home and umm, umm I'm gonna take care a him and our house and our eight babies! An, I'm never gonna hafta go to work." The four-year-old attacked her Cheerios with her usual determination.

Mommy said, with an odd look on her face, "Well, that's nice, Allie, but maybe you'll want to work sometimes. Sometimes mommies like to work, you know. For now, let's get you to daycare and me to my job. Mrs. Henderson will pick you up after school, and she'll feed you supper, too. Don't you love her suppers? I'll bring you back home in time for your bedtime story."

Birthdays Passed

The year Allie turned seven, Ted and his family moved to another state. She cried on and off for a few days. Mommy sat with her each evening while she cried, and they watched TV together.

More Birthdays Passed

Alice stormed into the house and plunked her books down hard. She started making supper.

Mom got home at six. "Thanks for cooking, Sweetie. That smells so good!" She looked closely at her daughter. "What's wrong?"

Alice frowned. "Those stupid . . . Mom, I didn't make the cheering squad. I am *so* bummed."

Mom hugged her shoulders, looking vaguely relieved. "Allie, I am sorry. I know you wanted that." She wiggled her daughter's shoulders just a bit. "But, you know, this will give you time to focus more on your studies. It would be hard to keep high grades and do cheering squad, too. I'm so proud of how well you do in school."

"Yeah, I know." Alice pouted through supper.

High School Passed

"A scholarship to State? Allie, that's wonderful! Will you go to State? You could live at home then, and it's an awfully good school. If my promotion comes through, maybe in your second or third year you can move into student housing if you want. But just maybe. You know we don't have much."

"It's OK, Mom, I know. We'll make it. I'm going to work at the library again this summer, and maybe I can get regular hours working there while I'm in school."

Halfway through supper, Alice said, "Oh, Mom. Emma, Ted's cousin, told me that he got a scholarship too, in football. He's going to Cornell."

Graduations Passed

Alice graduated from college and worked her way through law school. She became a public defender and eventually a judge.

"Hi, Mom. How are you feeling?"

"I'm doing all right, Sweetie. The new medicine is helping. How's work?"

"Oh, it's good. It's hard sometimes, you know, but that's OK. Hey, guess who I ran into the other day—Ted."

"Ted Collier? Is he living back here now?"

"He lives in Cleveland. He was visiting his aunt and uncle, and I saw them at the Chinese restaurant. He's talking about moving back here if he can find work. He washed out at Cornell, you know—leg injury and grades not high enough to stay—and says he doesn't feel that he has much of a career. He works in sales and seems to be doing well. He, he looks good, Mom."

Months Passed

"Mom, Ted and I have decided to get married. I'm so happy!"

"That's great Allie. If you were here, I'd give you both great big hug!" Mom teased, "So, Sweetie, are you going to have eight children and be a stay-at-home mom?"

"Whatever gave you that idea? Maybe a kid or two someday, but if anyone's staying home, it'll have to be Ted. I have a career to manage."

Figure 45 Photo Les Walters

A School Experience
Fran Cecere

This is not an experience that happened in school. It happened outside, however it left an impression on my mind and I can still see it happening, like a movie in my head.

I attended Utica Catholic Academy in Utica, New York. It was an all-girl school with an impressive reputation. The site of the building was on top of the highest hill in Utica.

Our parents worked, and could not drive us to school and there were no school buses, so my best friend, Dottie, and I had to take public transportation. The morning bus stopped right in front of my house so every weekday Dottie came to get me. The school was so far away that we needed to take two city buses to get there. We quickly learned what time the bus arrived at our stop, where we got the transfer to the second bus, and the schedule for the return trip home. If we were even one minute late for any of the buses, we missed them and had to run four blocks to a different bus line. The morning trip dropped us off at the bottom of the hill and we had to climb sixty-two steps to get to school before the bell rang.

After school we met our public bus at the bottom of the hill. It also ran on a strict schedule. No matter if there were inches of snow in freezing weather, it would not wait for us. That meant that we stood outside for half an hour with no shelter before another bus arrived. We did this crazy schedule every school day for four years.

Because we were in Catholic School, we wore uniforms that consisted of a white blouse, gray blazer, navy blue pleated skirt, white knee socks, and black and white saddle shoes. The skirt could be no shorter than the middle of our knees. If the nuns or the Priest, who was the Principal, thought the skirt was too short, we had to kneel down and confirm that the hem of the skirt touched the floor.

We hated the long skirts so as soon as we got outside, we rolled the waist of the skirt up a couple of times so the hem was above our knees. We did this while holding our books, and running down the 62 stairs to the bus. There were eight girls who took that bus and we raced and laughed as we took off.

One winter day it had snowed. There was a light cover of snow on the stairs and on the grass. Dottie said, "Let's not take the stairs. Let's run on the grass. It's much faster." I stayed close to the hand rail by the stairs but Dottie took off about six feet away from me. She hadn't taken two steps when she fell flat on her back. Her skirt immediately flew up over her face and as she tried to push it back down, she dropped her books one after the other.

I stopped running because I was laughing so hard. She looked like an out-of-control sled, but she got to the bottom much faster than I did. Still sitting down she called out, "Get my books." I started picking them up and heard her yelling, "Hurry up, the bus is only a block away." I tried to run faster sure that I would miss the bus. But then I realized all of the girls took their sweet time getting onto the bus so that I would not miss it.

Dottie and I sat together and relived the whole scene. We laughed all the way home but both of us were so glad that it was an all-girl school and no boys got an eye full of her white cotton panties.

It's Too Cold
Leilani M. Worrell

I am six. I chase after my big brother as he tries to ditch me. He's embarrassed he has a little sister who always tries to tag along. When I get too close, he stomps through a rain puddle and kicks his feet. The water sprays behind him and soaks my jeans. I give him a dirty look and head for home. It's too cold to be out in wet clothes.

I am twelve. As I enter the classroom, Kathy and her crew look up. I scurry to my desk, willing myself to be invisible to them. Too late. Kathy says loudly, "Hey, I like your dress. Is it new?" I mumble under my breath it's a new dress, and Kathy continues, "Where'd you get it? I might like to get one." Caught off-guard, I stupidly tell her the truth: it came from the thrift store. Guffaws fill the room as Kathy's gang explodes. I lay my head upon my desk and try to hold back the tears. It's too cold to learn anything.

I am nineteen, running downhill on an icy sidewalk to catch the bus to work. My stride grows too long, and my foot skids out from under me, causing me to fall heavily on my opposite knee. Righting myself, I see my pantyhose are ripped and my knee is bleeding into my shoe. It's too cold to even cry. I have to get to my job.

I am thirty-three. It's my first day on a new job. My boss, a career woman dressed to the nines, strides out to my desk. She slams down a bunch of papers and shouts, "What is this shit you gave me?" I look at the papers, then at her, and before I can answer, she orders "Do it again! And this time, do it right!" As she stomps back to her office, the man in the next cubicle says to not take it personally: she acts that way with everyone. But it's too cold to process what he's said, and I remind myself I need this job.

I am fifty-nine. I finally have an epiphany. I make little difference to the world in my present occupation as a civil servant. I am sad it took this long to realize. I am tired of it all. I consider the cold I've endured and decide it's enough. I am through.

I am sixty-seven. Now retired, I am comfortable in my skin, confident to see I'm the only one who knows what's best for me. I treasure my few true friends and urge my enemies to sleep with the devil, knowing karma is real. Time has taught me the importance of lessons learned from my father. Believe in yourself. Stand your ground with your head high. You are either your best friend, or your worst enemy. Don't start fights, but if they come, you damn well better finish them. Bring it on.

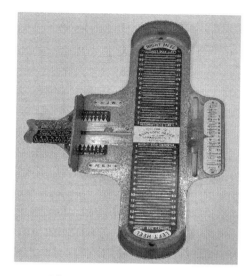

Figure 46 Photo Fran Cecere

If the Shoe Fits
Nancy Rice

Ah, the yearly shoe shopping trip. We remember the procedure —sitting on a grown-up size chair, feet dangling, and Mom picking out sturdy oxfords and maybe black patent leather Mary Janes to try on. We stood on that business-like silver and black gauge —a kind of slide rule for pedal extremities— to get the ever-changing measure of our feet. The sales associate, straddling that small piece of portable furniture common to all shoe stores, would whip out a shoehorn, slide the foot in, and expertly snug and tie the laces with fingers flying.

Then the ceremony began in earnest. Concentration, experience, and curiosity joined in the quest for a perfect fit. The importance of this endeavor was in inverse proportion to the age of the young customer. Goldilocks' formula was applied rigorously — it had to be just right.

Then the standing test with much pressing of juvenile toes through the leather. Next the walking test with a focus on

185

comfort and heel slippage. Finally, we approached the high altar of this ritual. A wooden cabinet about the size of an antique radio console housed a scientific marvel. The youngster stepped onto a low shelf at the base of the cabinet and inserted both feet into a small cavity under the mysterious works inside. Bending over the top of the cabinet and looking down through a viewer, he could see the outline of the shoe, the foot within it, and the bones of the foot —in glowing shades of green. Watching the skeletal toes wiggle in that ghastly palette was just icing on the cake.

Having achieved perfect knowledge of the foot in relation to the shoe, we gladly abandoned guesswork. The young foot could achieve its healthy adult size and function without any risk of harm from a shoddy shoe fit. This nirvana was only possible through the medical miracle of the x-ray.

However, at some point in the 50's, it probably dawned on people that Marie Curie's fate might offer some intelligence on the casual use of radiation for young flesh, blood and bones. Very quietly and quickly the foot x-ray disappeared from shoe stores forever. Clerks and parents returned to guesswork, imperfect but safe.

Ten years later, proper fit was not on the minds of the clients at Baker's Shoes. We were adolescent and female, and we came without moms to buy stylish flats for $5 a pair. We walked through the glass corridor between enormous display windows and entered to buy shoes that insulted the very notion of fit. The once-cosseted toes were jammed into a space bearing no likeness to the natural shape of the foot and high heels increased stress for the marvelous engineering on which we stood. It appears that these instruments of torture, not the foot x-ray, are the real threat to female foot health, only surpassed by foot binding in the deformities and difficulties caused. We were martyrs to style.

The shoe doesn't fit, but who cares?

SEASONAL

The fragrancy and colors of each season are portrayed in their full splendor.

Figure 47 Illustration Michele LeBlanc-Piche

Spring
Caryn Moya Block

Spring
Like a timid maid,
You peek from behind the frozen tundra.
A shy glance,
A smile, and a ray of your loveliness.
Oh, how we long for you to dance for us.
How we long for your fragrant scents
And vibrant blooms.
I see you peeking.
Come dance with me.

Spring
Haiku

Allita Irby

'Tis Spring with blossoms.

Mother Nature gives us gifts.

We thank Her for all.

Figure 48 Watercolor Laurie Rokutani

Spring 2
Caryn Moya Block

The pines are dancing

The leaves ring

The seedlings are twirling

As we celebrate Spring.

Figure 49 Illustration Michele LeBlanc-Piche

The Constant Gardener
Gail Matthews

Recently I was pulling weeds that grow between the paving tiles that create a landing at the bottom of the back porch steps.

Some weeds have shallow roots and are easily removed. Some run for many feet spreading as they go. Others will break off at the top, and the roots must be dug out, or the top portion that is left must be deprived of sunlight to eventually kill the plant. The latter takes vigilance on the part of the gardener as well as patience for this is a long process.

Some ideas are promptly discarded. Maybe they are allowed some space to blossom but are easily and quickly released. Some ideas like the runner grass invade outward. Today they are mainly carried on social media or television.

Those ideas, especially if hyped, seem to grow much faster than good news. They insidiously attack our lives and culture. Then, the ideology becomes rooted deep in racism, greed, injustice, discrimination, and hate. Love and faith can exist alongside but, if unattended, can be blocked out by toxic ideology.

As gardeners of humanity, we must be ever vigilant and refuse to provide the support that fuels negative ideologies. And we must plant the good seeds by constantly raising the banner of love, compassion, and belonging.

July

Bruce Van Ness

Seething weather that makes you melt

Course it's never Mother Nature's deliberate intent

Because puddled remnants of her tearful lament

May cool afternoon's sauna heat

Steaminess wraps so tightly against the skin

It squeezes last vestiges of stinging sweat

That burn the eyes and smear the sight

Even sparkling pools are quiet, deprived of their sanctuary relief

Bodies baste under the scorching breath of sun's savage glee

Rambunctious children flee inside

June premiered this seasoned heat and August will soon follow

Perhaps the breach of autumn air will be September's bravado.

Figure 50 Illustration Jen Poteet

Forest Floor
Jen Poteet

Growth new and old cushion our feet

Making footsteps hushed voices among us

The creak of swaying trees and rustling of hidden creatures.

Today you are a forest.

Yesterday you were the bottom of an ocean

Filled with long ago monsters.

What will tomorrow bring?

You hold the beginning of new life

In a seed and feed the hungry with flesh.

A circle never ending.

Gathering

Gwen Monohan

Where's my guiding compass,
plus map of all fall travel plans?
When bright colored leaves drift down,
I seem to breathe this restlessness.

Not unlike our wilder geese,
the ones still participating.
As they band together,
charting vast courses, navigating.

Seeking grain, filling those empty crops.
Engaged in honking conversations.
Hikers flock toward higher trails too.
Forging ahead, packs full.

Figure 51 Illustration Jen Poteet

No One There

Leilani M. Worrell

Weeding under the shrubs higher than my head
Rustling, rustling noises from above.
I seek my husband's form striding down the path:
No one's there.

More rustling, this time lower,
Oh, it must be my dog wanting attention,
I peer down the step-stones lining the path:
No one's there.

Now slithery sounds directly over me,
I gaze upward in apprehension, fearing a snake;
A breeze wends its way through the leaves, but
No one's there.

Still the whispering seems to call my name
I take in all the views I can manage
Trying to see in all directions at once, yet
No one's there.

Now bothered, worried, anxious
I take a deep breath and gather my logic
And at last the mystery is known
No one, but something there.

The trees that tower over the shrubbery
Cast aside their summer finery
In a gravity-driven wind-blown fluttering
Autumn is here.

Leavings

Gwen Monohan

Weeping cherry first.
Golden narrow wisps
sticking to moist bricks
like shavings from some fruit:
Apple, pear, or peach.

When not yet damp,
they scattered with a broom.
Making a yellow trail
to line the walk
like rows of flattened blooms.

Then came the oaks.
Brown before they dropped.
Like gnarled and wrinkled hands,
they landed in heaps
and piled-up about the steps
as though a heavy snow
had fallen in the night
and must be mounded.
Then raked again to tarps
and dragged to woods.

Now they've all come down.
Some ground by mower blades.
More hauled away.
Make way for new spring leaves.
Weeping cherry first.

Previously printed in *Second Wind*

Figure 52 Photo Les Walters

Meltdown
Gwen Monohan

Worn snow decays into
hollows
and seeps of the field.
Tan foam lines this road
beyond our barn.

Mounds, like aged glacial
debris,
moraine parking lots
in town with half lives
of their own.

The heavy fall-out,
making even the

moonless sky glow,
is cautious about leaving

this raw March day,
long past most groundhog's
cloudy predictions or
our almanac's review.

Soon spring-peepers will
call,
a more useful guide
for pale showers and late
cleansing of the green

Previously Printed in *Blueline 1999*

NOTIONS

Perspectives about truth, women, life, world views, the moon, generations, word choices, treasures, and compost.

Figure 53 Photo Fran Cecere

Everything Old Is New Again
Fran Cecere

My mother left me a treasure trove of old things. I always thought I would sell some of the items on Ebay. When I was still working, I didn't have time to put things on the internet, but now I have more time. When I saw how many records mom left me, I started researching what they were worth. I guess I waited just long enough for records to become the "new" thing.

People have started buying record players. I was never much of a visionary and I have to admit I did not see this phase coming. I lived through records, tape recorders, boom boxes, eight tracks, and CDs. Then MP3's hit the scene but I never owned one of those. It is also popular to have a play list on your phone. That trend snuck up on me and actually passed me almost unnoticed.

However, I have to say that the return of the turn table caught me entirely by surprise. I actually still own one, but haven't used it in years. Now my grandson wants to buy a turn table for his girlfriend and I am considering letting him have the one I own. I don't know if the needle will be any good though.

What will I do with all the vinyl records I have? He really is not interested in Bing Crosby even if it is the White Christmas album. I researched it and found out Crosby's first release of that album was in 1945. I don't think my album is that old. It was so popular it was released several times over the years. It originally sold for $17.99 but a first release album now sells for about $80.00. Should I sell my album? Good question.

I also have 45 RPM records. I remember buying an Elvis release for 99 cents when I was ten years old. It could sell for up to $1000.00 if I was lucky. I had a turntable that was in a little red case. It had a lever that moved to accommodate any size record. I don't know where that is now. I sold it in a garage sale many, many years ago. An original Elvis record now sells for up to $8000 depending on the title, the condition, and market at the time.

If I had the time to sell all the records I have, I might have enough money to buy lunch. It would take a great deal of time to make sure I got the right price for my collection. What I need is a young entrepreneur who is willing to do all the research for me for a share of the profits. Maybe I'll just find a buyer and take whatever he offers.

Truth and Reconciliation
Allita Irby

Apartheid...1950s Johannesburg South Africa
Discrimination...1950s Baltimore, Maryland USA

What is the Truth?
What is the Reconciliation?

Let not the oppressed become the oppressor.
Rise up.
Rise above the oppression.
Your lives matter.

Ignorance
Allita Irby

Ignorance has no color, no gender.
Racism has no color, no gender.
End ignorance, end racism.

Small State Life – 1970
Gary Misch

"The state is so small. Do you Rhode Islanders ever mistakenly drive out of the state?" The lady was being funny, or thought she was. There are few native Rhode Island comedians, though we do have a Cartoonist Laureate. The lady was from one of those big twang states out west, where they made more than adequate use of their 'R's, especially the ones at the ends of words. She probably thought the state was a few car lengths wide, and that we ended up in Massachusetts or Connecticut every time we missed an exit.

One disoriented tourist, crossing over from the Connecticut border, pulled off on the second exit ramp to grab a bite to eat. Imagining himself to be in a fully urbanized state, he hoped for a MacDonald's, or even an Appleby's. Instead, he found himself in our "Little Appalachia," an agricultural sector that time forgot, populated by men in overalls with few teeth and crooked smiles. The only restaurant was a small, local, very greasy spoon. The waitress spoke a curious dialect. She bore no pen and paper to take his order and simply said "whatz yawz." When he asked for a menu, she sort of gestured with her elbow toward a smeared blackboard behind the counter. "Anything good?" He asked. "Qwahg chawdah," he thought he heard. "I'll have that," he replied nervously, and had to admit that the odd concoction of clams, potatoes, broccoli, and onions in a clear broth was pretty tasty. On the way out he heard "See yiz laytta."

Many visitors arrive with the impression that Rhode Island was one itty bitty flat piece of black top running from Westerly at the southwest corner to Burrillville in the north. The fact was that until the recent orgy of building Rhode Island was mostly agricultural. There were three cities where the population was concentrated, but the lion's share was farmland and woods.

I spent most of my non-school youth either on Narragansett Bay, or on a farm in Adamsville with an old family friend.

She had come over from Poland before World War I, sailing in steerage on the Lusitania. She and her sister worked a small farm, with a little help from their cousin, who milked the cows and did some of the heavy work.

Rhode Island has always been heavily balkanized. A 1921 National Geographic ran an article titled *Rhode Island: Modern City State*. Things haven't changed much. When I was growing up, the French Canadiennes dominated the north, the Italians the middle, and the Portuguese the mid-south. The Jews and the WASPs were sprinkled throughout. The WASPs would have you believe they came over on the Mayflower, but there weren't many of those down here. The state was founded by a Puritan minister who was thrown out of Massachusetts for his radical ideas on salvation, and told to never come back. He became the first Baptist in America. Rhode Islanders have been considered troublemakers ever since. We prided ourselves on being the first big time smugglers in the New World, insisted on declaring independence from England early on May 4th, 1776, and refused to join the union until threatened. Oh, and we don't like dairy in our chowdah.

They say things have changed up there. We'll see.

Choices

Bobbie Troy

we make choices
throughout our life
but somehow
in the grand scheme of things
those choices seem puny
and insignificant
because they are
obscured by
fate or destiny
or karma
or whatever you want to call it

but we must continue
to make those choices
and try to guide our life
as much as possible
in spite
of the unknown
that lurks
around every corner

Figure 54 Photo Bobbie Troy

We Need to Believe[2]
Bobbie Troy

we need to believe
in something
that we cannot touch
or feel emotionally
something within
or without
that is beyond seeing
beyond doubt
because sometimes
what we have
just isn't enough

---

[2] Originally published 3/26/18:
https://cavalcadeofstars.wordpress.com/2018/03/26/bobbit-troy-20/

Just a Number

Nancy Rice

I am a number, not really an object, more like an idea. At the simplest level I am used to express quantity. Symbols, fingers, hash marks, even repeated noises, tell others how much, how much more, how fast, and how high.

I am a particular number—the number one trillion. I am easy to say—only two words and three syllables. I am easy to spell with only 11 letters. I am easy to write—the symbol for one followed by twelve symbols for naught, nothing, zero. And lately a lot of people say and spell and write me and multiples of me as if I were a simple idea. The trillion word falls trippingly from many tongues. Well, I am simply composed, the symbol for a single thing and the symbol for nothing. But these simple things are put together in such a way that understanding my size is a herculean task.

Here's one way to look at one trillion: I am one million millions. I am one million squared, or a million to the second power. Hmmm. This isn't working very well. That really doesn't show me in all my multiplied magnificence.

Perhaps we should try to understand a lower number, like one million. Let's pretend we can save one million dollars every day until we have $1,000,000,000,000. Oh, this is going to be fun!

We already know how many days that would take: one million days of faithfully banking that daily $1,000,000 at the local savings and loan. Now we're getting somewhere. At least we should be able to get a solid grip on the million thing and maybe even come close to comprehending the trillion thing.

All we need to do now is figure out how many years a million days is. Dividing a million days by the 365 days in a year, we get, in round numbers . . . 2,740 years? Oh, dear! That's no help at all. We'll never live long enough to save one trillion dollars that way. More than two millennia would contain over 30 lifetimes of average lifespans (79 years) end to end, not overlapping.

Peace
Allita Irby

Without Faith,

without Courage,

there is no Peace.

Keep the Faith.

Keep good Courage.

Imagine Peace,

if you can.

Imagine Peace,

for every man.

Novel Virus

Allita Irby

Not a novel book.
Not a book like a novel
but a new virus.

Figure 55 Photo Caryn Moya Block

One Sure Orb
Jan Price

Why do we love the moon?
We do.

Does it take us somewhere else?
Or bring us back to where we belong?
So far away down here alone.

Alone like the moon, perhaps we relate,
The moon up there, far away.
Close enough, so we depend
On the moon to bring us light,
A sense of joy, a feeling right.

When all around is dark out there,
One sure orb greater than the light
Of each shining star, however bright
Sometimes blurred through mist and fog
Yet pure and simple as we wish life was.

On nights when the moon may seem gone,
It's still there and will live on.
Go out, look up each night above
Inspired by the moon, live on as it does.
Strive and thrive, be there, shine forth

Count on the moon we love
Because.

My Lumbee Bodega
Allita Irby

Here we go again, I thought to myself. The last time I was in the small business office in Lumberton North Carolina, I checked the race box labeled, "Other", and wrote in, **Lumbee Nation**, on my retail license application. The clerk at the desk innocently looked up at me and replied, "Indians are extinct, Sir." So I left the office dumb-founded, perplexed and confounded. *How can you say that, lady, I'm standing right in front of you?* I took the license form and left the office with a headache.

Today, when I returned to present my small business application, I checked the "White" box, the "Black" box and the "Hispanic" box. I left the "Other" box blank. Another female clerk looked up at me and smiled, "You've got to pick one, Sir. You don't look White. You don't look Black. Hispanic?"

"Yes!" I said, before any other discussion could take place.

"Done!" She said as she stamped and dated my application with a self-satisfied smile.
"Good luck," she offered without looking up.

"Thanks," I said, as I thought, *Indian Tacos! Coming to a place near you, lady!*

Previously printed in *America 2020 Anthology by Riverside Writers*

Figure 56 Illustration pikisuperstar/freepik

Faceless Women of the World[3]
Bobbie Troy

we are your mothers, grandmothers, sisters, daughters
we are your wives, mistresses, and slaves
we have been revered and feared
by friends and family
often at the same time

we are your backbone, comfort, and peace
we are your adventure, shelter, and soul
we have been loved and hated
by friends and family
often at the same time

we are a force, a wonder, an enigma
we are open, free, and fearless
we are ignored and loved
by friends and family
often at the same time

---

[3] Originally published 7/24/17:
https://cavalcadeofstars.wordpress.com/2017/07/24/bobbie-troy-16/

we are hope, love, and happiness
we are brightness, spirit, and optimism
we are cherished and forsaken
by friends and family
often at the same time

we are the sun, stars, and planets
we are morning, noon, and night
we are seen and unseen
by friends and family
often at the same time

we are the faceless women of the world
marching on through time
forging our destinies and yours
as we go on
and on
and on

Sisters, Mothers & Daughters with Pockets
Alitta Irby

"Sisters with Pockets"
Sisters, fill your pockets
with all the knowledge you seek!
Fill your pockets
with all the love you need.
And then, give it all away.

"Mothers and Daughters with pockets"
My great grand momma had a pouch
with seeds in it.
My grand momma had a pocket
with chicken feed in it.
My mother had a pocket
with a driver's license in it.
I have a pocket
with a credit card in it.
My daughter has a pocket
with a mobile phone in it.
My granddaughter has a pocket
With a tablet in it.
What will my great granddaughter have in her pocket?

What does your pocket hold?

Previously published in *"America 2020"* Anthology by Riverside Writers

Figure 57 Illustration Gail Matthews

From the Tree of Knowledge - (What Lies Beneath)

Gail Matthews

A leaf pile is much like the experiences of life: brilliant yellow, passionate crimson, challenging orange.
Some are still green, plucked too early. Others are brown, spotted, torn, crushed.
Swirled on the wind, swept up in a pile, they lie layer upon layer.
Those closest to the earth feel the weight—the baggage—pressing.
The coolness of the moist, ground—a fresh start—calling.
Each layer, each experience eventually succumbs, only a memory.
But from all the layers, the soil is enriched,
and from the experiences in life, a kind of wisdom is born.
From that compost, comes fruit—new life, resourceful thinking, different directions.
This is what lies beneath, waiting.

Allies
Allita Irby

With Allies you can
fight evil in Europe and win a war.

With Allies you can
fight enemies foreign and domestic.

With Allies you can
fight for equality.

With Allies you can
fight for civil rights.

With Allies you can
fight evil in America and survive.

Figure 58 Illustration Michele LeBlanc-Piche

If You Were Me
Allita Irby

If you were me, you'd see what I see.
If I were you, I'd be different and new.

If I were you and you were me,
You'd sadly, gladly take a knee.

On bended knee,
you'd pray for the day we'd all be free.

March and Dance
Bruce Lugn

I awoke this morning to the news that Russian troops and tanks were marching into the nation of Ukraine. I foresee the end of dancing in Ukraine and possibly elsewhere for a period of time to come.

Rejoicing in life has turned many to sorrow and death. We shall see the battle, the destruction of human life from our couches as we watch CNN or NBC or Fox. The people of Ukraine will witness the battle on their doorsteps, in the subway shelters and perhaps from the grave. I shudder to think that only nights before some folks were dancing to lively music which touched their hearts.

As a child I would play cowboys and Indians with my neighborhood friends. The cowboys would march on their imaginary horses and shoot their weapons made of sticks and broomsticks or just use their imagination. Those who reluctantly would play the Indians would fall. Then they would ask to change places on the next round of the game. The cowboys might resist, but some would relent, and the game would begin in earnest again with much shouting, firing, marching, falling, and dying.

We would then be called by our moms—Dinner is ready was the evening call. The voices of the mothers could be heard across the neighborhood. We would reluctantly scatter toward our homes where we would find a table set, warm food and questions from our parents about our day and play.

On some evenings, my older sister would turn on the radio or put an album on the record player and we would hear the latest hits of Elvis Pressley or the Beatles. We kids might dance, or at least move parts of our bodies, attempting to find a rhythm that worked for us! Maybe the dance would be in our minds, like a dream. But a parent might then ask, "Is that music? Let me play Benny Goodman or Count Basie or well why not Beethoven or Bach?"

Now dancing to Glenn Miller or Count Basie seems like a wild thing to do even today!

This morning I turned on CNN and witnessed the dance of evil which is invading Ukraine. I see the tanks and soldiers marching. Maybe marching is a kind of dance. But it is a dance of danger to life. That dance is not life-giving. It is a dance of lies and corruptions and waste. Wasted lives that held so much promise to the mother and father at birth. "Oh, my boy will grow up to be an astronaut, or my daughter will grow up to be an astronaut. Or my child will learn to live with loving kindness." The dance of life.

The Truth
Bobbie Troy

the truth
sometimes stands
in our midst
like an unmovable pillar
or hangs over our head,
cloud-like and threatening

we think we can see it
or feel it
sometimes
we're not quite sure
of what it is

but it's there
if we choose to look

Answers[4]
Bobbie Troy

there are no answers
only people who think
they have answers

---

[4] Originally published 8/24/12: http://voxpoetica.com/two-by-bobbie-troy/

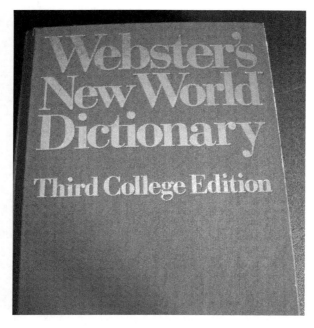

Figure 59 Photo Fran Cecere

Changing Merriam Webster's Dictionary
Fran Cecere

There is one word in the dictionary that I feel should be completely eliminated. I will give you an example. Let me know if you can pick it out from the reading and if you agree. This is only one of the many actual conversations I heard on television.

Picture a beautiful professional woman aged 25 to 30. The women could be an attorney or a wedding photographer. She is on a show where she could find the man of her dreams. He offers her a glass of wine and wants her to tell him about her life.

She has a very serious look on her face as she explains, "Like I had a like very sad life, like, like a mother who was like a big drinker like every day. Like she left the like family when I was like ten years old. Like she like never came back and like my dad was like cool but like I missed my mom like every day. My sister like took off like shortly after mom like left. I like never like learned to cook and like dad and I ate like canned food all the like time. In like High School I was like large and like the boys teased me like a lot. I didn't like have many like friends, but like one girl got to like know me and like brought me to her like home and her mother like helped me face like puberty. Like like this woman helped me to become the like woman I like am today. I like went to like college and like got a like degree and I like am ready to have a like family and like children. I like really have like feelings for you. I like would like to continue on with this like relationship.

I have to stop now. I can't stand to see it on paper. When I watched it on TV, I counted 60 times she said the word. I only used it 50 times. I can't image living with her and pity any children she influences. It makes me sad to hear this type of conversation. Should we remove the word from the dictionary? Would these women or men know how to talk if they couldn't use that word.

I'm glad I do not have to deal with this in real life because I think I would have to put my child into time out every day. I would do whatever I had to do to stop this hideous habit. Anyone want to join me?

IN REMEMBRANCE

*Honoring lives
well-lived.*

Figure 60 Photo Sally Humphries

Culpeper and The Young George Washington
Sally Humphries

Be sure to meet George Washington, the young surveyor, the next time you are in Culpeper. His bigger-than-life mural is painted on the outside of a building at the corner of Main and West Cameron.

Here's the back story of George's early years:

Augustine Washington, his father, took him into the tobacco fields to hoe weeds and kill tobacco worms at a young age. No one could supervise workers until he knew the job himself, was the parental viewpoint.

Augustine, a tobacco farmer as well as managing director of the nearby Accokeek Iron Furnace, was also a determined educator. Using the principles of the Appleby Grammar School in England, he had George start most days with an hour or two of lessons before breakfast. Augustine's small farm office was the classroom where George studied alone.

All of this changed when George was eleven and his father died, leaving his mother in charge of his three younger brothers and a sister. The role of mentor/teacher fell to his older step-brothers, Lawrence and Austin.

Both lived nearby, and Lawrence had married into the Fairfax family, one of Virginia's largest landholders. George thus had access to the extensive library of Lord Fairfax, and it guided his education. An interest in mathematics led to the study of surveying which, in turn, led to George's first on-the-job experience.

The oldest Fairfax son and George were invited to join an experienced surveying party for a month-long trip across the

Blue Ridge Mountains to explore the vast Fairfax land holdings. According to George's diary, the first day began with a forty-mile horseback ride, ending in an overnight stay with a frontiersman.

George might have looked forward to a restful night, but instead he found his bed to be "a little straw matted together . . . with only one threadbare blanket" and "double its weight of vermin, such as lice, fleas, etc." As soon as the light was taken away, "I put on my clothes, and lay as my companions (on the floor)."

Another night he bedded down in the open air next to the campfire. Peace and rest lasted only until his straw bed caught on fire. It was the beginning of his learning experiences as a frontiersman.

According to historian, James Thomas Flexner, in those thirty-one days of blustery March and April, "he swam horses across a river swollen by snow melting in the mountains, met a party of Indians carrying one scalp who, when inspired by a gift of rum, performed a war dance; [and] got lost in the Blue Ridge Mountains, where he encountered a rattlesnake. He found it all exhilarating."

He also decided to pursue surveying as a profession. It was a good decision.

The Fairfax land holdings in Virginia dated from 1649 when King Charles II of England had deeded five million acres in the northern part of his colonial empire to loyal supporters which included the Fairfax family. Through death and marriage, the land was consolidated under Lord Thomas Fairfax, who was now headquartered some four miles upstream from the home of George's brother, Lawrence. Lord Fairfax was impressed with the young man's work ethic, and the Fairfax-Washington connection began to flourish.

Ultimately, George was appointed County Surveyor for the newly created frontier county of Culpeper. The year was 1749 and George Washington was seventeen years old, a teenager by today's standards, but a young man of valuable service and promise in the 1700's.

Otho William Helm
Gary Misch

Otho William Helm, known to his fellow lodge brothers as Bill, was born on 30 January, 1922 in Roanoke, Virginia. At age 15 he left school to apprentice on the Norfolk and Western Railroad as a brake man on the coal trains running from Bluefield, West Virginia, over the mountains to the port of Norfolk. Brakemen were in line to become conductors. It was not an easy life. Bill would tell of winter days and nights sheltering in open cupolas on coal drags running over the Blueridge at 15 to 20 miles an hour behind double-headed steam engines belching smoke and cinders.

As much as he thought he wanted to be a railroad man, Bill got off the train one day in Norfolk, and headed for the Navy recruiting station. In a few months this boy from the central Shenandoah Valley found himself stationed on a cruiser in Pearl Harbor. It was February, 1941, and he thought he had embarked on a remarkable adventure.

On 1 December Bill's Ship got underway with the USS Enterprise battle group to deliver fighter planes to Wake Island, and possibly search out hostile Japanese forces. Fortunately, the battle group never found the Japanese. The American force was much inferior to its Japanese opponent, and almost certainly would have been destroyed. That Japanese force was on its way to attack Pearl Harbor on 7 December.

Here is where Bill's story takes a turn. In 2002 the Department of the Navy belatedly presented Bill with the Pearl Harbor Medal, which was awarded to those American servicemen who were impacted by the Pearl Harbor attack. Bill had applied for the medal in 1942, but had been turned down since his ship had been underway. But Bill and four other members of the deck department had been left behind at Pearl Harbor with the ship's boats. They had been in the attack, and participated in rescue efforts in the aftermath. Someone in the Department had finally consulted Bill's ship's deck log and discovered the names of those sailors who had disembarked prior to sailing, and so Bill was finally presented with the award he had earned all those years ago.

Figure 61 Photo Sally Humphries

Betty Washington Lewis
Sally Humphries

What would it be like to live in the 1700's and have a big brother like George Washington? Betty Washington took it all in stride. She was only a year younger than George and had three small brothers.

Her father, Augustine Washington, had died at age 51, when Betty was ten. The Washingtons owned chunks of land but no glittering silver tea services, no coaches or carriages. Augustine had been a tobacco farmer as well as managing director of the nearby Accokeek Iron Furnace.

He strongly believed in education and made a special trip to England to learn the principles of the Appleby Grammar School for his young sons. Betty learned to sew, knit, embroider, dance, ride a horse, and be a housekeeper which was the custom for girls at that time.

When her cousin, Catherine died shortly after the birth of her third child, Betty was there to help. It wasn't too long before she accepted the proposal of Catherine's widowed husband, and at age 16, became Mrs. Fielding Lewis with a ready-made family of two stepsons.

Fielding, age 24, was the younger son of a very successful merchant and was soon managing the family retail store in Fredericksburg. In a short time, he was able to buy 1,300 acres on the outskirts of town and employ his brother-in-law, George Washington as a surveyor.

Meanwhile Betty was busy birthing eleven children, six of which survived to adulthood. Fielding was active in the vestry of St. George's Church, the House of Burgesses (1760-8), and was appointed a Colonial in the Spotsylvania militia.

For a time in 1765, Fielding helped administer a school for the children of enslaved African Americans. There were sixteen students until opposition developed and enrollment dropped to four. Fielding was forced to close the school during the winter of 1769-1770.

By July of 1775, George Washington had been named Commander of the Continental Army and was tasked with keeping the British bottled up in Boston. The Lewis family began sending supplies to meet the needs of Massachusetts patriots.

The Virginia Assembly set up a "Manufactory of Small Arms" using public funds to equip the Continental Army with muskets, rifles, and cannon. When public funds ran out, the Lewis family used their own money, borrowing against their assets.

The Lewis's retail store became the main source of salt, flour, bacon, and clothing to Patriot troops while Betty's vast garden supplied teas and ointments.

Fielding's ongoing battle with consumption (tuberculous) ended his life two months after the American victory at Yorktown in 1781.

As a widow, Betty struggled financially. The Commonwealth of Virginia owed her 7,000 pounds but had nothing but worthless paper currency to offer. George was equally hard pressed, being land rich, but cash poor. He had to borrow money to travel to his own inauguration.

Betty's financial problems continued. She tried running a boarding school out of her home and sold some of her land to meet expenses.

Finally, after fourteen years she came to Culpeper to live with her daughter, Betty Carter. Illness ended her eventful life in March of 1797 at age 64. Today her Culpeper gravesite is maintained by the DAR Minutemen Chapter.

Some Prayers Are Wordless
Rose Lyn Jacob

In March of 1965, the Reverend Dr. King called for religious leaders of every denomination to join the Selma to Montgomery March for voting rights. One of those answering the call was Dr. King's close personal friend and passionate supporter of the Civil Rights Movement, Rabbi Abraham Joshua Heschel. They walked linked arm in arm along with other religious leaders, Black and White, from all over the United States.

When Rabbi Heschel returned from Selma, he was asked the question, 'Did you find much time to pray, when you were in Selma?' Rabbi Heschel's response? 'I prayed with my feet.'

Rabbi Heschel's words taught that the task of repairing the world requires not only *appeals* to a higher power, it requires ACTIVE prayer. His marching, his protesting, his speaking out for Civil Rights was his greatest prayer of all.

On the third Monday in January, we observe Martin Luther King Day (MLK's Day). It is a Federal holiday created to honor the life and work of the Reverend Dr. Martin Luther King, Jr. It is unusual for Americans to honor an individual with their own Federal holiday.

George Washington and Christopher Columbus are the exceptions. The traditional way to honor these two historical figures is to hold nation-wide sales.

However, the traditional way to honor Dr. King is with a Day of Service, making time to volunteer and to engage with your community. This honors the legacy of Dr. King with actions that speak louder than words alone.

It took a long time and a lot of hard work and grass roots petitioning to bring MLK's day to fruition. The campaign to create a Federal holiday in Dr. Kings' honor began soon after his assassination in 1968, but it was not signed into law until 1983, by then President Ronald Reagan. One of its greatest, most vocal advocates for MLK Day, was the singer and musician, Stevie Wonder who went on a national concert tour to drum up support for the MLK Federal holiday campaign. In 1980 Stevie Wonder wrote a powerful song for the tour. Here are a few of the lyrics:

"You know it doesn't make much sense
There ought to be a law against
Anyone who takes offense
At a day in your celebration 'cause we all know in our minds
That there ought to be a time
That we can set aside
To show just how much we love you
And I'm sure you would agree
What could fit more perfectly
Than to have a world party on the day you came to be."

It is almost unfathomable that, even though signed into law in 1983, it took until the year 2000 for all fifty states to officially observe the day.

Dr. King believed in the prophetic model of the Hebrew Bible. He had read many of Rabbi Heschel's books, including one entitled, "The Prophets." He understood that prophets often stood alone as they advocated for change and spoke loudly to condemn injustice.

In his prescient last speech, the night before he was assassinated, King said, "Like anybody, I would like to live a long life. Longevity has its place. But I'm not concerned about that now, I've seen the Promised Land. I may not get there with you. But I want you to know tonight, that we, as a people, will get to the Promised Land. And so, I'm happy tonight; I'm not worried about anything; I'm not fearing any man. Mine eyes have seen the glory of the coming of the Lord."

Jewish tradition teaches that: It is **not our** responsibility to **finish the work** of repairing the world, **but neither are we free to desist from it.** Let us pray that each of us finds his or her way to "pray with their feet," or their hands, their time or their voice to become actively vigilant in the pursuit of the peace, justice, security and equality.

Figure 62 Illustration Sally Humphries

July 4, 1776

Sally Humphries

It was a hot, steamy July day in Philadelphia, Pennsylvania. Delegates from the thirteen colonies were meeting to debate Richard Henry Lee's resolution for Independence. All appeals to the British king for a solution to England's oppressive tactics had been exhausted. It was time to fish or cut bait.

There was to be one vote per colony, as decided by the majority of the delegates present. When the roll was called the New York delegation declined to vote either way, saying they lacked specific instructions. The British had been counting on a "no" vote from New York, thus many independence supporters were encouraged.

The New York abstention was followed by surprising "no" votes from South Carolina and Pennsylvania, colonies where popular opinion favored independence. Delaware was a stalemate, with three delegates, one opposed, one in favor, and the third temporarily absent from the deliberations.

Virginia's Edward Rutledge moved to postpone the final vote on Lee's Resolution for Independence until the next day, July 2. This would give the Delaware delegation time to summon its absent delegate, Caesar Rodney. Rodney was a strong supporter of independence, but had been called home to squelch a pro-British uprising. A courier was sent to tell Rodney the urgency of the situation.

The extra time would also give the South Carolina and Pennsylvania delegates time to reconsider.

The following day was dramatic. In the words of noted historian David McCullough:

" . . . it appears that just as the door to Congress was about to be closed at the usual hour of nine o'clock, Caesar Rodney, mud-spattered, 'booted and spurred', made his dramatic entrance.

"The tall, thin Rodney . . . appeared stranger still, and more to be pitied, by a skin cancer on one side of his face. He kept it hidden behind a scarf of green silk. Almost unimaginable, he had ridden eighty miles through the night, changing horses several times, to be there in time to cast his vote."

The roll call vote began again. Two of the Pennsylvania delegates who couldn't bring themselves to vote "yes" stayed away from the meeting, enabling their delegations to vote for independence. South Carolina gave in for the sake of unanimity. New York continued to abstain.

When Delaware was called, Caesar Rodney rose to say: "As I believe the voice of my constituents and of all sensible and honest men is in favor of independence, and my judgment concurs, I vote for independence!"

The decision was made. Twelve colonies were in favor of nationhood. The debate now began over the specific wording of the Declaration, and by the evening of July 4, the document met the approval of all. American Independence was born!

And now the rest of Caesar Rodney's story. When Rodney signed the Declaration, he not only put his life on the line as a traitor to the Crown, he also denied himself access to possible medical help in the British Isles. He never showed regret for his decision.

He continued to serve Delaware on committees, councils, and honorary positions in the militia. From 1778 to 1781 he served as Governor. What he couldn't do physically, he did financially— until his health forced him to step back.

He lived to see the surrender of Cornwallis at Yorktown in 1781 but missed the enactment of the Constitution, dying at the age of fifty-six at his home near Dover. He will always be known as a man of conviction who never gave up or gave in—regardless of the cost. A true champion of American Independence

The Colonel
Gary Misch

I met the Colonel in the 1900s. After Garland Meadows died, the Colonel began sharing counter duties with a lady at Graves Apple Shed Store in Syria, Virginia. I met him one day far into the year when business had dropped off. I was looking for cider. He was tall, a good six' five" I'd say, straight as an arrow, rail thin, with a high forehead, close cropped hair, and getting on in years.

He smelled of Army. As retired Navy, I could sniff out a Marine, and he wasn't one. That left Army. No Air Force guy would look that razor sharp in retirement.

I was wearing one of my many Navy ball caps, so he recognized me as a fellow military man, and we chatted often over the years. His name was Ervin Kattenbrink, from Tennessee, but Army travel or habit had squeezed most of his accent out of him.

Like everyone who minded the Apple Shed Store, the Colonel was a volunteer. I never understood what volunteers got out of their work, but the Graves must have given them something; volunteers tended to be long term "employees".

Like me, the Colonel had come to live in Syria from his last active-duty tour inside the Washington Beltway. He and his wife Jean, whom he had known since his days at West Point, which he pronounced WEST point, had one of the great romances of the 20th century. They lived atop a mountain, overlooking the valley. Their house included a fish pond, for she loved to fish, and he loved her with all his heart. If she loved to fish, she would have a fish pond.

The Colonel had seen her picture via a friend while he had been at the Academy. She had run into a burning building to save someone. He had written to introduce himself, but her parents thought it improper for her to date a stranger, even one acquainted with someone she knew. But eventually they came to know each other, fell in love, and had a life-long romance.

Sadly, Jean died of cancer in mid 1990s, and was buried in the Criglersville Cemetery, next to an empty plot where the Colonel would eventually join her. As far as I could tell, they were so much in love that neither was meant to outlive the other, but such is life.

I would often go bicycling, and end up at the store, talking to the Colonel. He would tell me about his life with Jean, his time in Vietnam (he had pictures), his admiration for Lou Gehrig (he had one of Lou's jerseys!), the fact that he played a small role in the movie "The Thin Gray Line" (he was actually on camera for several seconds).

He was a faithful New York Yankees fan; he seldom missed a game broadcast on his satellite TV, and they carried every game.

One day the Colonel was gone. He could no longer live alone. He had moved to a nursing home, but his days were short. It seemed that most of Syria and the surrounding area accompanied his body up the hill to be interred next to his beloved Jean. And there they will spend Eternity looking down together on the valley they loved.

IN MEMORIUM

*Late Authors
provide laughter,
wisdom, beauty,
loneliness and how
a dime can change
a life.*

Some Other Words

Figure 63 Photo Fran Cecere

Lavanda K. Woodall (1932 – 2017)

Calamity in Cade County
Lavanda K. Woodall

If there was ever a match made in heaven, it was Clementine Bean and Digger Jones. They fell in love at the Cade Methodist Church ice cream social last July and was married a month later at the same church.

Clementine Bean was Doc Henry Bean's old maid sister, Clemmie, as everybody called her, had come to live with Doc Henry and Mrs. Bean after her mama died. She was tall and skinny with red hair and a million freckles. Not exactly what you'd call pretty, but a sweeter girl never lived.

The groom's, Digger Jones, real name was Stonewall Jackson Jones. We called him Digger cause he was the official grave digger for Cade County. He was a short, thin man and real dressy. Why, you never saw Digger when he wasn't all spruced up with every dark hair in place. His brown eyes always had a sparkle, and he always had a joke for everybody. A more cheerful man you'd be hard put to find.

Right after the wedding, I asked them where they was going on their honey moon. Digger told me proudly they was headed for Paducah.

"You got family in Paducah, Digger?" I had to ask.

No, Ma'am. I just always wanted to go there." Digger was grinning at Clemmie who was blushing so much that all her freckles seemed to run together.

Well, it takes all kinds, and if Digger and Clemmie thought Paduch, Kentucky was romantic, who was I to put a spoke in their works. From looking at them, though, I don't think they'd know if they were in Paducah or Timbuktu.

Anyway, Digger and Clemmie left on Monday. By Thursday afternoon we all knowed we had a calamity in Cade County.

Tuesday morning Ina Mae Brown, who had enjoyed poor health since 1942, passed on. And Jesse Murcheson died unexpectedly in Florida and was shipped home that same Tuesday. About ten o'clock Ben Porter was driving down Main Street, lost control of his car, crossed the sidewalk and hit old Mr. Sewell a glancing blow. Then at twenty miles an hour the car went right on through the new plate glass window of Delbert Greer's Mercantile Emporium. It ran over two racks of men's casual medium size trousers before pinning Allie Sutter, Delbert's part time employee against the north wall. Well, it was touch and go for poor Miss Sutter for a time but the two racks of pants couldn't be saved.

Ben and Mr. Sewell expired of Heart attacks within the hour in the same room at the hospital.

To top it all off, Archie Doolittle's Aunt Elsie fell in Big Tilden Creek and drowned while trying to save her little dog, Poochie. Poochie, who had been chasing a neighbor's cat, was not a great loss, but Elsie Doolittle would be sorely missed.

Well, as you can imagine, this was a terrible day in Cade County where we usually lose one or two people a month.

Nowhere did it hit harder than at Mack Pearl's Funeral Home, where they was hard pressed to find room for all these people.

It was decided to put all three of the ladies in the larger Meditation Room. Although at this stage of the game, I can't see it makes a particle of difference who goes where.

This left Ben Porter and Ronald Sewell to share the smaller Quiet Time Chapel. Nobody was sure this would work, cause there was real hard feelings between the Sewells and the Porters. This all stemmed from the regional high school basketball tournament of 1938. And started when Ron Sewell stole the basketball from Ben Portrer and made the winning basket. Now this wouldn't have been so bad except they was both on the same team.

One thing about it though, it was good for business. The Starlight Motel was busting at the seams with all the out-of-town people here for the funerals. And the Rite Café had to hire two more waitresses.

Well, it didn't dawn on Zack Pearl or anyone else for a while that there wasn't anybody who could dig all those graves. After trying and failing to break into Digger Jones' padlocked cement block building to get his grave digging machinery, there was some frantic calls made to other nearby counties looking for a grave digger. One county's digger was gone to the Gulf fishing. Another said that he belonged to a union and couldn't work in Cade County. A union? What was the world coming to? Myrna Basset suggested we use Erwin Smith's backhoe, but it had been broke down for two months waiting for a part from the other side of the state. Finally, it was suggested that all of the families ought to get shovels and spades and start digging. Then it was discovered that the ground was solid as a rock. Nobody had thought about it, but it was August and we hadn't had a drop of rain in over two months time.

In the end Zack Pearl called a meeting of all concerned and laid out the problem. There was no way to get the graves dug until our own Digger Jones came back from his honeymoon in Paducah, Kentucky.

So Zack and his son, Bobby Lee, piled all those coffins in the back room at the funeral home and there they stayed until Clemmie and Digger came home the first of September. When they got home old Digger went right to work. It took a couple of days. Clemmie sat in a lawn chair about twenty feet away and watched Digger operate his backhoe.

Then all one day there was funerals. People just went from one to the next. It was a local holiday, you might say. Bernie Truitt suggested we do this every year. Everybody just laughed at him. But, you know, the more I think about it, the smarter it sounds.

Herbert F. Frisbie - (1925 to 2010)

Gifts
Herbert F. Frisbie

Of all the gifts to give a child, there is nothing that could be,
More wonderful or marvelous than teaching them to see,
And think and feel and dream about the wonders that surround,
And the mysteries of nature, that in the earth abound.

Bountiful
Herbert F. Frisbie

God granted us great Bounty
From the fruit trees that He made,
Though other trees may not bear fruit,
They give us soothing shade.

Days End
Herbert F. Frisbie

Silence seems suspended from the air.
Sunset paints a purple hue upon the quay.
Blades of grass and leaves all cease their timid whispers
As for a moment all things pause in gratitude
And quietly honor passing the day.

These poems were not in any of the earlier anthologies

Figure 64 Photo Fran Cecere

Judy Zummo – (1944 – 2021)

Learning to Sail
Judy Zummo

When I was a child, I spent every summer with my grandparents who lived in a cabin on the Chester River in Chestertown, Maryland. I had a ten-foot hand-made rowboat which could be transformed into a sailboat by stepping the mast and the sail. But I was content to row my boat, take my grandparents out and have picnics in the evenings on the river.

My grandmother always made deviled eggs and chicken salad, my two favorite things to eat. My best childhood memories are of the times I spent with them. My parents usually came down on the weekends with my brother and sister. We spent the days swimming in the river, catching crabs, and playing baseball.

One weekend, when I was ten, my mother decided it was time for me to learn how to sail. She assured me that she was an expert sailor and would teach me everything I needed to know.

On Saturday morning, she, my little brother in his life-jacket and I set out so I could "learn how to sail." Mom stepped the mast and hoisted the sail and off we went heading east. There was a gentle breeze, the sail luffed in the wind. We were sailing! She explained how she was able to steer the boat by changing the angle of the sail to catch the wind which controlled both the direction and speed.

We were moving along at a good clip and were having a grand time. My mother realized my freckled red-headed brother was beginning to get sunburned. This was before the time when people were aware of the dangers of sunburn and the importance of sunscreen.

My mother explained how we were going to "come about" and head back. She did manage to turn the boat, but we continued to sail east even though the bow was heading west. She tried everything she knew to do but we continued heading east at the same speed. She finally realized that we had been riding the tide, not really sailing. At the same time my little brother was getting redder by the minute. We covered him with towels. We had to do something before he blistered.

The river had little traffic so hailing another boat and getting a tow or ride was not an option. My mother suggested that maybe I should get out and swim. I tied the bowline around my waist, jumped into the channel and started to swim toward home. It was rough going as I was not only swimming against the tide but also towing the boat with two passengers. It was exhausting. I was finally able to get close enough to the shore where I could touch bottom and pull the boat rather than swim. The bottom was squishy over sharp rocks which were tough on my feet. But we finally made it back! We tied the boat.

My mother carried my brother and we walked back to the house. My little brother had blisters on his face and shoulders, and I was tired out.

From that time, forward, when my mother suggested we go sailing I declined the offer.

Bette Hileman – (1937 – 2020)

A Dime Provides
Bette Hileman

In 1970, my family was subsisting on welfare in West Los Angeles. My husband Sam and I and our children—three, four, and six—were living in a house we owned in a good neighborhood.

Sam had bipolar disorder, also known as manic depression. Two years earlier, in 1968, he'd quit his job as editor in the ethnomusicology department at UCLA to support the family as an artist and writer. I was qualified to work as a lab assistant, but after paying for childcare, a lab-assistant salary would provide nothing to live on. Sam was too unstable to hold a steady job or look after the children full time, but now and then made a few hundred dollars from selling paintings.

Welfare payments covered the mortgage, utilities, food stamp purchases, and most other expenses if we watched every penny. California's Medicaid, the most generous health benefit for the poor provided by any state, took care of doctor bills at clinics in excellent hospitals, such as UCLA's.

Before Sam quit work, we'd removed dingy wallpaper from every room in the house and painted them with beautiful colors. He had created fine oil and acrylic paintings that hung in most rooms. After he stopped working, we sold our car and gave up the telephone to save money. We did grocery shopping with bikes and made calls at a nearby phone booth. Because neither of us held a job and we lived in an attractive place, some neighbors thought we were rich and preferred to live like hippies, numerous in the late sixties.

The mortgage payments didn't include the real estate taxes. As time went on, the taxes rose, and when they came due in early 1970, we couldn't pay them. We needed three hundred dollars to avoid foreclosure.

My parents wouldn't help. They imagined that, if we found ourselves in desperate straits, I'd leave Sam, a positive step in their view.

Near the end of February, we had absolutely no money left. We looked under the sofa cushion and found one dime—the cost of a local call. Sam told me he was going to the phone booth to contact an editor friend, Jim, and ask for free-lance editorial work. He left the house.

When he returned, he was elated and incredulous. "I dialed Jim's number, but instead, I was connected with Ruth, who grew up five miles away from me in Goshen, Virginia. She's a social worker here in West LA. My father was her family doctor. He charged nothing to take care of her family because they were so poor. She's coming to the house."

A few minutes later, Ruth arrived and lent us three hundred dollars, which we repaid over the next few months. She told us that when she was a child during the early thirties, her parents had no jobs. To earn a little cash, they sold the meat, milk and eggs they produced on their small acreage. Primarily, she ate vegetables and fruit the family raised, a common practice in Appalachia. She lost all her teeth by age twenty.

Because of Ruth's trust and generosity and the sale of several more paintings, my family's financial situation stabilized somewhat. We staved off foreclosure and potential homelessness for two more years. Eventually, we moved to Sam's hometown of Millboro, Virginia, where I began teaching high school.

You could interpret finding help from a wrong number in a city with three million people as pure dumb luck or the hand of God or what goes around comes around. Whatever it was, those crossed telephone signals provided money that eventually led to college graduation for the children, recognition as an artist and editor for Sam, and a satisfying career in journalism for me.

Previously printed in: "In Other Words"

Figure 65 Photo Fran Cecere

MaryAnn Morrison – (1943 – 2017)

Thoughts
MaryAnn Morrison

Today the sun, blocked behind a wall of thunderous clouds, brings no warmth. Familiar sights and sounds filter through my thoughts, as I drag myself out of bed.

After all, it is a day just like many others. It is not a cold-shower day that brings one quickly back from a dream state. It is a day for a warm soak in the tub, releasing the body's stiffness and melting away fears. My morning rituals begin.

As I drink my juice, I think about people I see every day—strangers passing each other without notice, intent only on their own reflections.

I wonder which of them grabs a bagel along with the car keys that hang waiting by the door. How many of them are lucky enough to gather around the breakfast table, nourishing body and soul while giving thanks for the day and each other before entering the fray of a constantly spinning world.

Suddenly, I realize how quickly time has passed as the radio interrupts my reverie. "The clouds will be heavy all day," says my favorite weather expert. I pick up my sunglasses anyway, not sure if I am indulging in wishful thinking or just trying to hide the searing pain of loneliness reflected in my eyes.

Printed in "Words Across Time"

Figure 66 Photo Fran Cecere

Renate Ruzich – (1926 – 2020)

Beauty Beyond Imagination
Renate Ruzich

It was a summer, not too long ago, that I was on my way to judge a horse show in Arizona. The flight had been late and I had a three-hour drive ahead of me. After renting a car, I hurried to arrive on the Mesa between the Zuni and the Apache

Reservations in daylight. Having worked there before, I was looking forward to this weekend.

After a half hour's drive on the big turnpike heading west, my car suddenly started to stutter and then stopped. After just making it to side of the road, I checked the water, the oil, the temperature, but found no problems. So, I put the hood up as a sign that I had trouble, but nobody stopped or even slowed down. A police car went by on the other side, but it seemed that everyone was concerned to get home. I waited and waited, knowing that the long drive ahead would keep me from arriving at a decent time this evening. I tried to call someone but everybody must have been at the show grounds.

So, I waited and waited in that awful heat without even a breeze to help. Luckily, I had some cold drinks with me. All around me were bare hills and not a spot of shade in sight.

After almost an hour a young man with a rickety farm truck stopped.

"What's the trouble? This is no place for you to be alone."

Yeah, tell me! After explaining what had happened, he started to check the motor, the water pump, even crawled under the car to look for leaks. Nothing.

He offered to take me to the gas station and lunch room on the reservation where I could call the car rental company. I was a bit leery to go like this, with a young Indian man, but I had to get to the show.

The place was not far and the people were really nice and helpful. They worried about my having been so long in the heat, standing by the highway. They brought me cold tea and the owner gave me his phone to use.

Luckily, the rental office was still open and sent another car and a tow truck for the disabled car.

The lunch room owner had been about to close for the day, but decided that I should not wait outside alone. So, they stayed open to wait with me for the new car to arrive. I was so thankful to them, after all those others had passed me by.

Sometimes one finds the most wonderful people when in trouble. Was I ever lucky!

The car came. We checked the radiator, the brakes, the oil, and the gas so I could safely leave. I thanked my new friends profusely, and they refused any other payment for helping me.

Off I went. The road I had to take went south after getting on the Mesa and was only a small State Road. The trouble started when it got a bit darker and I wanted the headlights. No luck. I hadn't asked how to turn them on.

A lot of wildlife crossed the road and I realized that the end of this trip would take even more time because I had to drive slowly. Checking the lights was the one thing we had not done. Maybe that hot sun had cooked my brain a bit.

Now the sun was setting with unbelievable color. The western sky had light misty clouds and the whole sky was drenched in all the reds of the pallet, a solid tent of colors. They got deeper and brighter by the minute. The whole western horizon and the sky above me was covered.

Having stopped to take this all in, I had paid no attention to the eastern sky, but then I turned and there was the moon. It was gigantic and the color of a ripe orange with the dark grey of the coming night as background. The scene was so large and intense that the moon seemed as near as the mountains below it.

There was no way that I would miss a second of this whole show, no matter how late it got. I was awe struck. This was such unbelievable beauty, so unreal, with colors that I had never seen or even could have imagined.

So, I stopped and just sat there letting this time take me off to wherever. There are no words that could do it justice. This huge moon slowly rose and became less intense until long after the sun's last sliver had slipped below the mountains.

There I sat for a long time until it was dark. For the rest of the miles, I drove like in a dream. It was a slow trip without headlights and it seemed that every creature around had to cross this road tonight. But I did not care. I just got to my motel and left a message for my contact.

The show was great, the horses did a lovely job, and all the trouble the day before was nothing compared to the beauty I was permitted to see.

Previously printed in: "In Other Words"

Biographies

Caryn Moya Block is an award-winning author known for her twenty-five paranormal romance books. She has also published four children's and one non-fiction book. Several anthologies have published her poetry. To learn more about her, please visit www.carynmoyablock.com

Brown Cardwell traveled the world sharing her artistic talents. She taught dancing and singing, was a playwright, director, actor, and member of the Screen Actors Guild. She wrote two books: *Jericho* and *The Scroll of the Fourth Wise Man*. Now she writes poetry and is active with Windmore's writing group.

Fran Cecere wrote stories throughout grade school and college while earning her Master of Science degree in Nursing. Her involvement with Windmore includes being: a facilitator of the Pen-to-Paper Writers' group, past president of Windmore, and acting with their community theater. This is the fourth anthology she has helped Windmore produce.

Bruce Clark has spent many years writing as a part of his occupation as an attorney but is new to creative writing. He started to write as an outlet following the death of his wife and hopes to expand his skills over time.

Sally Humphries, a career journalist and Phi Beta Kappa graduate of DePauw University, has a passion for the stories of people in America's history. She also has a calico cat and writes "Cally Tales," a monthly newspaper column that gives insights into Cally's life as a cat.

Allita Irby is an avid reader and book lover. She has been writing seriously since 1995. Her writing has appeared in many anthologies and online journals. She enjoys writing women's fiction, flash fiction and poetry. Allita also writes about contemporary issues and current events.

Rose Lyn Jacob is a free-range rabbi living in Syria, Virginia where she meets the spiritual needs of Jews in the surrounding five counties. She has turned her journalistic skills toward writing humorous but inspirational sermons, wedding vows and eulogies. Rose uses stand-up comedy to entertain and break down barriers to understanding.

Michele LeBlanc-Piche is an artist. Her paintings directly reflect her heart's desire to reawaken, honor, and celebrate the innately Feminine energies of life. The aspects of love, intuition, receptivity, nurturing, healing, emotions, and all of Nature inspire and influence her creativity. www.heartexpressionsbymichele.com

Bruce Lugn is a United Methodist pastor. Bruce blogs at *www.hearingthedivine.com.* He is the author of *From the Heart: A wife's struggle with cancer, a husband's journey of love.* Bruce enjoys gardening, writing, and walking. He is married to Alessandra; they have four adult children and two grandchildren.

Gail Matthews has an M.Ed. with an emphasis in Instructional Technology from George Mason University. She is the webmaster for Windmore's site online. Windmore's last anthology, *In Other Words,* published her first stories. Gail used personal, *Unsplash, Pixabay, and Wikipedia* images with many submissions.

Gary Misch, a retired naval officer, lives in the Blue Ridge Mountains with his wife and seven cats. He enjoys fishing and rescuing cats and kittens. His writing, both poetry and prose, almost all non-fiction, reflects his life experience.

Gwen Monohan feels poetry is replenishing. She's had poems in Windmore anthologies, literary journals and online at Vox Poetica. She won 3rd prize in California Quarterly for "Focal Points" and 1st prize from Dover Beach Poetry Press for "Robin's Wake." Gwen is currently working on publishing a book of poetry.

Carolyn M. Osborne lives with her husband and pets on a forested mountainside facing the Blue Ridge. She writes historical narratives and is working on the fifth and final book of her *Helena's Stories* series. After that . . . who knows? There's plenty to research and write about.

Jen Poteet wears many hats: mother of teenagers (less predictable than dragons), homemaker, vintage enthusiast (you say hoarder I say maximalist), artist of many mediums, mainly of the permanent variety on skin. She really loves words so much she joined this writers' group to get better at using them.

Lois Griffin Powell attended Hampton University and Southern Connecticut University and has a Master's Degree in Writing. She has published three children's books about her main character Samantha and a young adult book, *Kesha and the Curse of the Artifact.*

Jan Price became a reading teacher after graduating from the University of Virginia. She did not realize how much of a writing teacher she would become. Along the way, she also taught herself. Jan writes mostly nonfiction, but poems occasionally seep in, becoming creations in their own right.

Nancy Jarvis Rice, an Ohioan, writes because she loves hammering words into concentrated meaning. She says when she is writing, "Time just stops." She writes about memories of her happy childhood. She pays close attention to the national scene and writes about that as well. "It's mental exercise—always a good thing in moderation."

Laurie Rokutani is a watercolor painter who loves to play with light and impressions. Her latest "experiments" involve allowing the paint to create the picture, a process of discovering what wants to emerge rather than starting with an image and producing it. Laurie paints for the pure joy of painting!

Bobbie Troy maintains sanity and perspective on life by writing poetry, flash fiction and original fairy tales with a 21st-century twist. However, she is best known for her poetry. Her work is published widely online and in some print anthologies. Bobbie's first poem was published when she was 62.

Bruce Van Ness has three previously published novels: *My Run for the Presidency and Other Assorted Crap*, a political satire; *The Gospel Truth*, a blending of biblical prophecy with the secular trappings of earthy life; and *Vignettes from the Twilight of Life*, an older man's treasury of memories and reminiscences

Les Walters is a retired Lieutenant Commander from the USN Nurse Corps. He is a former nursing instructor for Germanna's nursing program. For Windmore anthologies, Les has submitted photographs for the stories and the book covers.

Leilani M. Worrell is a retired USDA Inspector with a B.S. in biology and a minor in geology. She wrote as a teenager and discovered her writing abilities through Windmore's writing group Pen-to-Paper. Leilani aspires to develop those skills further to share her unique outlook on life.